BETWEEN

LOVE

AND

GRIEF

M.M. MALDONADO

BETWEEN LOVE AND GRIEF

A Mother's Journey After Teen Suicide

This book contains content that can potentially be a trigger for self-harm, suicide, and death. Please use caution as you read or share this book.

You understand that this book is not intended as a substitute for consultation with a licensed practitioner. Please consult with your own physician or healthcare specialist regarding the material in this book. The use of this book implies your acceptance of this disclaimer.

If you feel suicidal or are having a mental health crisis, please call **988**.

Maria Martina loves hearing from readers.
Reach out to her by email at authorMariaMartina@gmail.com.

All drawings by Sofia Bella.
Photography by Sofia Bella and Maria Martina.
Cover photo by Czarlize Jereos.
Book cover and interior design by Linsey Dodaro.

Print Paperback ISBN: 979-8-9905506-0-5
eBook/ePUB ISBN: 979-8-9905506-1-2

DEDICATION

In loving memory of Sofia Isabella and all beloved victims of suicide.

I also want to dedicate this book to the suicide loss survivors, the ones who are left behind with the loss, the unbearable pain, and the many unanswered questions. May God bring the peace to your soul that you so desperately need.

Finally, I dedicate this work to my sister and my mom. Rosy and Lupe, my heart is full of gratitude. Your unconditional love, your faith, and your prayers were like a warm blanket that soothed my soul when I needed it the most.

"There is no limit to how complicated things can get on account of one thing always leading to another."

E. B. WHITE, FROM CHARLOTTE'S WEB

 TEENS - many of you will experience depression or anxiety at some point. Most of you do not fall into the thinking that suicide could be an option to deal with the situation because it is most definitely NOT a solution. When comparing the number of teens with depression and anxiety disorder who go on to live productive lives, the number of those who don't are minimal. Yet, any life lost to suicide is precious. YOUR LIFE IS WORTH LIVING!

TABLE OF CONTENTS

A VERY SPECIAL TYPE OF BOOK

I always wanted to write a book. I had many topics in mind but never in my wildest or scariest dreams had I thought I would write a book related to death, let alone suicide. That was not my expertise or life experience. I am a Child of God, a daughter, a wife, a mom, a pharmacist. I am many other things, but I am no expert on suicide or dealing with grief. This book is NOT an expert opinion on dealing with suicidal thoughts or grieving a death by suicide by any stretch of the imagination.

In the blink of an eye, I became that mom who lost a child to suicide. How could that be? Why? "*There has to be a purpose for all of this,*" I said to myself in between moments of disbelief, anger, and total heartache for the loss of my precious Sofia Isabella.

I know that God makes all things new. There is always some good that comes out of terrible tragedies if we wait and trust God to show us new paths out of the dreadful labyrinth of pain. I claimed as mine the cry from Romans 8:28, "*We know that in everything God works for (the) good with those who love him, who are called according to his purpose.*" Even when I knew that passage to be true, it was hard to find purpose while drowning in the high waves of the biggest storm of my life. Yet a little ray of light in my darkest moments led me to believe that everything was going to be okay in time.

This book started as a desire to publish some of Sofia Isabella's writings. She wanted to be a published author one day and this was one way to honor her memory. As I began collecting her writings on my computer, many questions came to mind. How does a girl filled with so much life and love get to the point of not wanting to live any longer? Then I got to her latest drawings and writings. They were dark, every sentence filled with pain, and bleeding out of the pages. They were a cry for help, but they were private. I only received access to them through her friends and when looking through her things after she was gone.

Sofia Isabella was caught between two worlds. The dark world inside her mind and the world around who loved her and fought against her to keep her alive.

As I continued the process, my writing was telling a bit of her story by me commenting on what she wrote. My grief was on display and my motherly heart wanted to be able to help others. I then felt that I was the one in between two worlds: Love and Grief. The world where I was dedicated to her and loved her in all the ways I knew how even after her death and the aching grief of losing her and thinking about what else could I have done to save her. That is how this precious book came to be.

I am honoring Sofia Isabella's memory by joining the voices that bring awareness to Suicide Prevention. I feel she will want that and it will make her proud. I will accomplish this through her writings, my grieving, and sharing some of my experiences as a suicide loss survivor. In this, I found a purpose for the senseless loss of such a gentle soul.

Through his love and mercy, God changes broken things and people into new and beautiful creations. In revealing parts of her story, maybe a ray of light will shine over someone needing a word of encouragement or hope.

Like I said, I am no expert, but I lived through it. I am a suicide loss survivor, someone left behind to live with the consequences of a death by suicide. If anything in this book, such as her poems or my words, can help bring clarity, ideas, hope, or perspective to the topic of suicide prevention, I will consider that we, Sofia Isabella and I, accomplished our goal. If someone can be rescued from suicidal ideation due to anything presented or any resource in this book, that will be God's way of saying to me, "*Well done good and faithful servant*". My soul will rejoice knowing that something good came out of her tragic death, for the glory of God.

The first part of the book is dedicated to suicide awareness from a mom's heart and as a friend who wants the best for teens suffering from this hideous plague. In the second part, I will share most of Sofia Isabella's writings and some stories providing deeper insights into her life. You will see happy writings at the beginning that will open the door to her precious caring heart and mind. As we move forward, you will start seeing her anguish and pain surfacing. I will also share how things progressed. It will be a hard thing to do for me since I will share very private stories to bring light to a difficult subject.

I hope that in sharing this way, you will get a front-row seat to our story of love, pain, and grief as Sofia Isabella lost her battle with mental health to suicide. It is my prayer that in reading some parts of our story, you will be able to benefit by having better knowledge on the subject to prevent a tragedy in your own family or those under your care. If the tragedy already happened, I pray that this book helps you understand a little better what happened and find some comfort and peace knowing that you are not alone.

 Insight: Sofia Isabella was the name that Steve and I gave to our baby girl. Over the years, we came up with many nicknames for her, these are a few of them: "Sofi, Sofi Bear, Truffles, Bella, and Isa". For the most part, we called her Sofia or Sofi. Her sister called her "Mocha," and Uncle Scott called her "Baby Goose". She went through a phase during fourth and fifth grade where she asked her friends to call her "Applejack" or "AJ" like one of the characters from *My Little Pony*. Some of her grade school friends called her "Sofifi".

When Sofia Isabella transitioned into High School, she started introducing herself as Bella. I asked her once, "*Do you want us to call you Bella now?*" She responded, "*I am good with my family calling me Sofia but new people should call me Bella.*"

Throughout this book, I mostly refer to her as Sofia Bella to honor her wishes as well as the way we always call her. Sometimes I will use one name or the other. She was a very artistic and creative girl; one name was not enough for her and we loved her for that.

Written in June 2022

My funny, smart, and ever-creative Sofia Bella;

You left us behind. I've drowned myself in a pile of details and information trying to put the pieces of your life puzzle together. How did you get so sick in front of my eyes?

How is it that I was not able to recognize how vulnerable you were that day thinking that you just needed some space when you mumbled with a so familiar *"leave me alone"*? You were showing so much progress at that time. Why, even after all we did, we were not able to rescue you from yourself?

Why did you refuse to follow your safety plan? Why did you call your close friend instead of calling the hotline? Why didn't your friends text me to watch over you like they did other times when they realized that you were losing the battle against your ill brain? A perfect storm was brewing with the sole purpose of depriving the world of your gentle soul.

Why didn't you tell me that night what was happening before I left for the airport? Why didn't I see that you were struggling when I went to say goodbye and you didn't want to look at me curled in bed? I was so used to your rejections at that point and thought nothing different regarding you not wanting to speak with me.

Did you think about any of us before you did what you did? Were you desperate and wanting to go fast? Or was it something that came slowly and naturally as a thought would come to mind?

I want to believe that if you understood the depth of our love for you, it would have given some light to your darkest hour. If you could feel the love of many who knew you, loved you, and wanted you to be well you might still be with us. Yet your mind was too sick to engage in those thoughts, find any hope, or figure out a path forward to deal with the enormous pain you had in your soul. I know I will only get answers when I see you again in Heaven, my little angel.

In trying to make sense of things, I've been in the place where you took your last breath. It was scary at the beginning, but then it gave me some weird comfort. It helped me imagine myself supporting you as you drifted away. Did it hurt? Did you struggle? I embraced your imaginary self as if you were still there. I was comforted thinking that you drifted into the arms of Jesus. I imagined him taking you by your hand, after a long embrace, and saying, "*At last, YOU ARE BACK HOME.*" In going through this, I cried and ached so deeply but I also found relief.

Other times, I screamed and called your name out loud to relieve my pain. As time goes by it is getting better. I am so grateful that I have a strong sense of God's merciful love. It is what keeps me going and makes my pain more bearable. I can only offer this pain to God in hopes that I can pave my way to Heaven and see you again sooner.

By the way, when I see you in Heaven will you run to me? Will you want to hug me then? Or will you look peacefully my way and with your ever-enchanting smile say, "*Oh yeah, that's ma*'" while keeping busy with your heavenly duties? Who knows? I do KNOW that I will be running towards you and giving you the biggest hug ever in the history of Heaven. We will embrace for the longest time while angels sing around us sharing in our joy.

You are now gone from my sight but soon we will be together forever.

Love,

Ma!

PART ONE

Mental Health – A Topic for Everyone

INTRODUCTION

Opening the Door to Talk About Suicide

A s I write this introduction, I am faced with many questions. Why me? Why do other kids with depression and anxiety disorders end up getting better and living full lives? Why did my Sofia Bella have to die? How did she decide that death was the only option?

When all those questions keep creeping into my thoughts, I am left with one truth, one answer, the only answer: my Sofia Bella was very ill. Her sickness made her do what she did.

Sofia Bella loved life and was intrigued by all things, big and small. Her love for the things and people around her did not prevent her brain from developing a type of depression, combined with an undiagnosed number of other related mental diseases, that was comparable to having a terminal condition. Only by looking back and reading more about mental health am I able to begin to make some sense out of it although there is never a clear explanation. Her mental illness, even under treatment, put her in a position that no one was able to get through and save her. She locked the doors to all possible help and threw the key away.

At the time, I did not know this. I was consumed with trying so hard to be there for her, to negotiate with her about therapy, hospital stays, and many other attempts to make her well, and happy, while keeping her alive. Unfortunately, not even my motherly love and thousands of prayers from family, friends, and even strangers could save her. You can't love someone out of terminal cancer just like you can't love them out of the equivalent in the world of depression and mental illness. This is not to say that we won't try with every fiber of our soul and every minute of our waking hours. God still performs miracles and many have been saved from such circumstances.

My daughter died of depression with a high component of anxiety by suicide. This is not to simplify the fact of her death or romanticize it, as there is nothing romantic about death by suicide. This is me, accepting what happened and knowing I did everything I could to avoid the fatal end. This is me sharing my heart to hopefully help someone else from despair.

A suicide joke is made

They laugh like it's no big thing

Inside, I am thinking

About that one time

That I tried to kill myself

About that one time

The cut went so deep

It would not stop bleeding

About that one time

I laid on the floor

Sobbing and wishing I'd die

Curled up in a ball

Written By Sofia Bella. No title or date. Found on a note-book with 8th-grade school content

CHAPTER 1

Effects of the COVID-19 Pandemic

on Mental Health

L et me start by talking about the elephant in the room in a more specific way: mental health, suicide, and the COVID-19 pandemic.

In 2021, the American Academy of Pediatrics declared a state of emergency concerning children's and adolescents' mental health. That alarm did not surprise many of us living through it. Unfortunately, the number of suicides per year is still high. We need to continue educating the public on the subject and on how to help prevent suicide.

Why do we need more education? Talking about mental health and suicide is still perceived somehow as an obscure, unpleasant, *"I'd rather not talk about it"* type of subject. Many of us want to change that.

In a CNN article published on April 25, 2022, author Kristen Rogers discusses the results of a study suggesting that adolescents' suicides increased during the pandemic based on data from five states in the United States.

Provisional data from CDC's National Center for Health Statistics indicate that both the number and the rate of suicides in the United States increased by 4 percent from 2020 to 2021, after two consecutive years of decline in 2019 and 2020. For 2021, suicide deaths increased by approximately 5% in the United States. The provisional number of suicides in 2022 (49,449) was 3% higher than the final 2021 number (48,183). The age-adjusted suicide rate in 2022 (14.3 deaths per 100,000 standard population) was 1% higher than in 2021 per the data provided by the Center for Disease Control and Prevention under Provisional Suicide Deaths in the United States, 2022 released on August 10, 2023.

 Insight: More than 50,000 Americans died by suicide in 2023, a number higher than any year on record, said Kristen Welker in a special edition of Meet the Press. The U.S. surgeon general calls mental health the "defining health crisis of our time."

Here is another data point from JAMA Pediatrics 2022, Science Update: Youth suicides increased in the first year of the pandemic. The National Institutes of Health, known as NIH, funded a study looking into the effects of the pandemic and suicide. The study reported that *"the stresses of the pandemic may have contributed to an increase in adolescent suicides"*. When combining data from 14 different states, researchers saw an increase in the number of suicides among youth 10 to 19 years of age and in the proportion of youth suicides compared to the overall population.

When combining data from 14 different states, researchers saw an increase in the number of suicides among youth 10 to 19 years of age and in the proportion of youth suicides compared to the overall population.

The COVID-19 pandemic robbed us of precious lives lost to the actual virus. But there was also a huge amount of grief and pain caused by missed experiences. Students missed many milestone events such as graduations, birthdays, school dances, school concerts, speech team competitions, cheerleading trials, theater play auditions, art exhibits, sports trials, and games that all could have led to life-changing scholarship opportunities that were now lost. Even just the opportunity to hang out with friends creating significant memories and shared experiences was gone due to lockdowns and social distancing. Fear became a "*normal*" state of mind. We were all constantly stressing and worrying about getting infected or infecting a loved one and putting lives in danger. At the beginning of the pandemic, it seemed justifiable. As time went by and more information started to surface, then it became a debate on who was right, who was wrong, and who had the power to make decisions. Squashed and wrinkled with these arguments, our adolescents were confused and a sense of hopelessness overcame many. Those already suffering from depression and anxiety were at a great disadvantage in navigating the emotions and trauma of such times. Hopelessness is one of the main culprits, if not the primary one, driving young people to suicide.

Some media outlets went as far as to call those who dared to come out of their house for fresh air "*murderers*", even though those people were just looking to combat their loneliness and lack of human interaction. Guided by multiple social media postings, our Sofia Bella fell into a similar kind of thinking. Many of her friends did as well. Their face-to-face interaction was minimal when they needed it the most.

Hopelessness is one of the main culprits, if not the primary one, driving young people to suicide.

All that fear was compounded by a 24/7 news channel's ticker with the number of deaths and hospitalizations in the US and around the world. This uniquely impacted our adolescents. Our teens were now isolated from their peers, hiding in their rooms, with a front-row seat to the greatest tragedy of their time coming live to them via their phone and tablet screens. It was very hard for all of us to experience. Can you imagine how it was for those who were already battling anxiety and depression?

Sofia Bella's father, Steve, and I realized we needed to do something. Sofia Bella was isolating even more. She started avoiding the family at all costs and was not even having meals with us. We resolved that we needed to disrupt the pattern and change the scenery. We planned a family road trip to South Dakota.

Sofia Bella told us that we were trying to get ourselves killed and that the road trip was a terrible idea. She was very nervous about going into nature to breathe fresh air even though we were going to have limited interaction with others. Setting her fears aside, we moved on with the plan and found a cabin in the middle of nowhere to stay at. Together, we created good memories and did our best to have fun and disconnect from the craziness of the pandemic. We saw her smiling again with a renewed love for nature as she hiked, drove past giant buffaloes, captured frogs after a rainy day, found a turtle, and got close to adorable prairie dogs.

Adolescence is a stage where teens are in most need of interaction, peer feedback, exploration, and other ways of discovering or confirming who they are and who they want to become. With isolation, all of that was lost. Some kids even regressed in their social skills by isolating themselves even more. Sofia became very anxious and could barely sleep. Teens tried to find refuge on their phones only to discover and open doors that brought a new set of problems. Isolation, desperation, hopelessness, unlimited access to mindless, and at times very harmful, TikToks and YouTube videos became the normal state of affairs for these young minds.

Trying to find someone to help us was extremely hard. Therapists' and doctors' offices were closed. Some were offering care via Zoom or similar virtual platforms. If I could place an emoji here, it would be the one with the two eyes wide open in disbelief. A Zoom type of session for a teen whose mental health is deteriorating was like a bad joke. "*Don't you understand that she needs to be seen by someone in person?*" I would say. "*I am so sorry ma'am; this is our policy. We need to keep everyone safe*" would be the response. In the meantime, we could go to Target, Walmart, and supermarkets. How could that be possible? It was insane.

Finally, we decided to start something remotely. It did not work. Maybe it worked for someone else, but not for us. Not for a kid who was unmotivated, hopeless, and anxious - already playing with the idea of suicide.

Hospital stays came soon after, but also with many restrictions.

I had to fight with the school to have Sofia Bella join a group of peers who were allowed to go to school and do remote learning in a supervised room. That got her out of bed for a few months. I felt hopeful.

There are a couple of lawsuits from parents of teens who died by suicide against local governments, claiming that coronavirus restrictions and lockdowns were responsible for their teens' suicides. One example of this is Lisa Mara Moore from Illinois. Her son died by suicide due to unbearable isolation and lost chances to practice the sport he loved. Sports and other social school events were vital for Mrs. Moore's son. She claimed that isolation made him a different person.

It is sad to realize that when we needed more mental health professionals in our schools, we used the COVID-19 relief money to isolate the kids even more installing shields around their desks instead of adding mental health resources.

To our youth, isolation damaged more people than exposure to the virus itself.

I will never know how things would have turned out for Sofia Bella without the COVID-19 pandemic. I know based on my experience that the government pandemic response certainly made things worse.

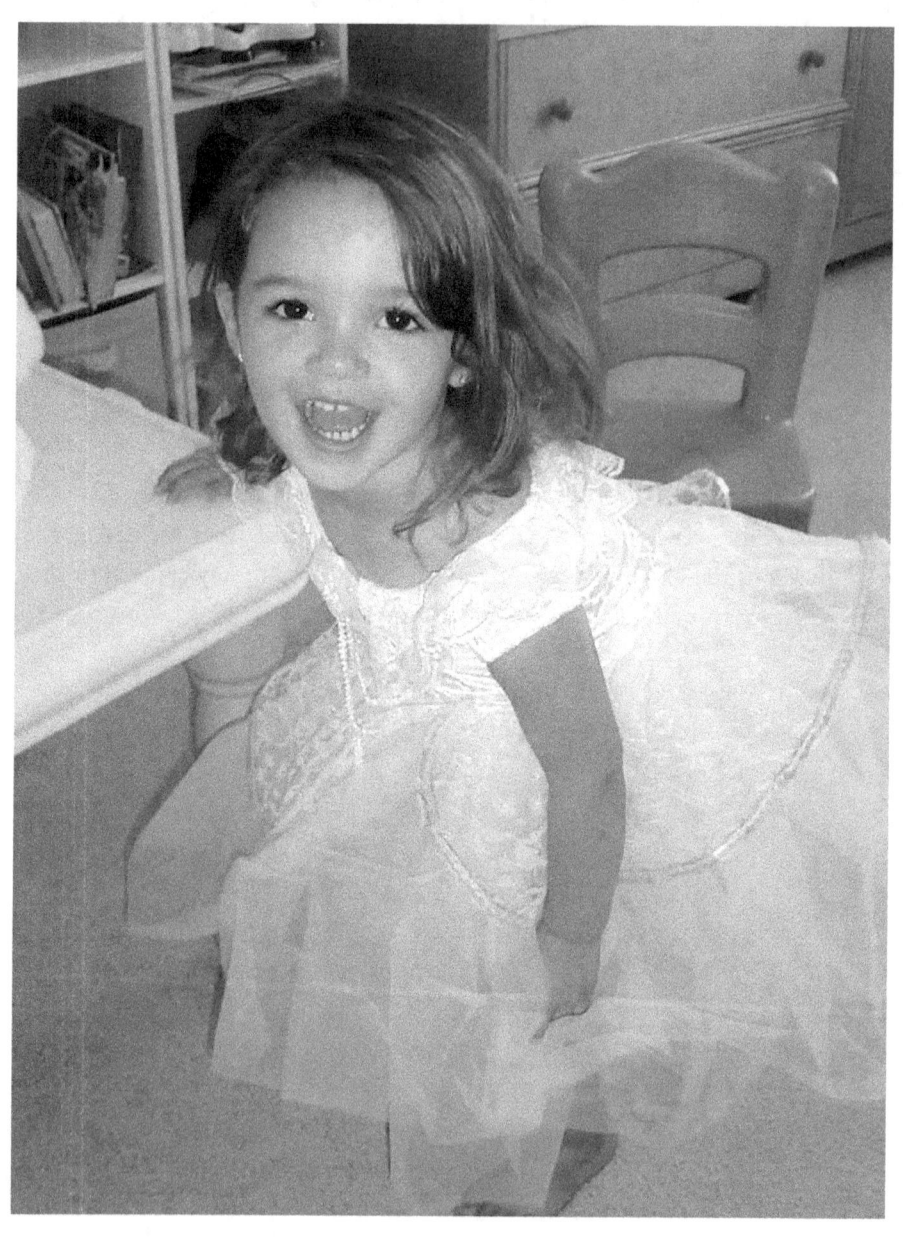

Sofia Isabella getting ready for her 3-year-old birthday party.

CHAPTER 2

It Can Happen to Anyone

A Happy Little Girl

When Sofia was a little girl, she always thought of herself as a princess. She loved to dress up and the best gift you could give her was a pretty dress. She would wear that dress over and over again. She twirled around the house with her pretty dress and fake heels. She was the princess of our home.

I remember one year towards the end of Halloween; I bought all the princess costumes I found. They were all at 50% off. I bought a big chest and for that Christmas her greatest gift was a pretty chest filled with princesses' dresses and accessories. She was the happiest little girl on the block. She was loved and she knew it.

Time flies way too fast. Soon she became a teen. It is not easy being a teen, especially in our times. For our kids, it must feel like being a green frog in a swamp full of brown frogs. We are all awkward, but the green frog feels like he is the worst for being green. What he does not realize is that what makes him different makes him also so special. He becomes sad and anxious. All he wants to do is to be like the other brown awkward frogs.

It is not easy being a teen. It is awkward, plagued with
insecurities, and a roller coaster of emotions.

No matter how good of a family and environment a teen has, going through this stage of life is one of the hardest things a person will experience. It is awkward, plagued with insecurities, and a roller coaster of emotions.

Sofia Bella was raised in a good home. I halted my career to spend more time at home supporting her and her siblings as needed. Like any other mom, I encouraged my kids to read, do well at school, bring friends home, and get involved with extracurricular activities. I was driving them to sports practices, games, school activities, and birthday parties. My favorite part of the day was when Sofia and Daniel would come home from school. I would have food ready for them and would try, many times unsuccessfully, to engage them in conversations to learn about their day. I miss those days.

Sofia's dad was and is a hard-working father. Steve's parenting style included respect, discipline, and a good work ethic. At the same time, he was playful and funny. He would read or make up stories at bedtime and always finish up with prayers. Prayers and reading stories ran well into middle school. It was their routine. In high school, they would listen to music and play the guitar. Eventually, Steve bought Sofia Bella her own guitar and later a keyboard as she grew more interested in music and theater. Steve took Sofia Bella to many Father-Daughter dances, taught her how to roller skate, change a car tire, check the car engine's oil, and many other things. Was he a perfect dad? No. I was not a perfect mom either. Who is? Did he lose his patience with a hardheaded teen? Absolutely! Overall, those two loved each other in their unique way.

Sofia had a curious mind and was eager to learn many things. She was physically strong with a very sensitive mind.

We both encouraged Sofia's love for horses by buying her all kinds of books about horses. She knew her horses very well. Her dream was to have a horse of her own. We nourished her imagination for writing stories and poems. I encouraged her to think about publishing her writings one day. She loved that idea.

Sofia Bella had an older sister, whom she admired. Her sister loved her dearly. I loved it when Sofia's sister was old enough to take Sofia shopping for school supplies and Christmas presents for the family. They always had such a good time together and most of the time it would end with them going to eat at Noodles and Company or similar as they were both pasta lovers. With a 12-year age difference, big sister was either away in college or working for most of Sofia Bella's middle school and high school years. There was a year between her sister's undergrad and grad school when I had all three of my babies in the house. It was a full house. My heart was happy. It was also a messy and loud time trying to deal with the needs and expectations of a college graduate, an almost middle schooler, and a grade-school little boy. At times it was hard and with Steve working so many hours things were even harder.

Sofia Bella also had Milo, her doggie companion. Did I mention that I never wanted to have pets in the house? Milo came to our family after Sofia insisted that she wanted to have a dog. One time I tried to convince her that a fish was also a pet. She looked at me with puppy eyes saying, "*But I can't hug a fish*". That melted my heart and opened the door for Milo. Milo was her longtime friend and also her therapist. They took long walks at times. I recently discovered pictures and videos of Milo in the basement or her room. Places that were banned for Milo but were frequented while we were not home. Those two were inseparable.

Daniel is Sofia Bella's younger brother. He was her little playmate in many of her silly games. Five years younger than Sofia, he was her target when she needed to vent. He was also her little servant when she needed something. Daniel was bossed around when Sofia wanted to have authority over someone other than Milo. Daniel always complied with her requests as he wanted to be in his sister's good graces.

We were not a perfect family by any means. We loved each other and tried to live our family life the best we could, falling short many times. We tried to be good to each other just like many families I know. Through the ups and downs of family life, we also knew that God was with us and He loved us.

Her early years were fun and filled with love, adventure, and learning at Abbott's Bright Horizon Day Care. She started Kindergarten at Saint Patrick School in Wadsworth and graduated from 8th grade at the same school in 2019. While at school she learned more about the love of

God and his love for all creation. Sofia Bella loved all things Jesus and frequently would talk about and describe with awe and joy what would it be to one day go to Heaven.

Our home, her school, and church were safe places for her. School was her second home and her classmates were her second family rivaling her best friends from the neighborhood, Czarlize and Arriana.

Her extended family was very present in her life and enjoyed spending time with her. Sofia Bella visited Florida and Puerto Rico many times just to be close to her cousins and the rest of the family. Sometimes she went with us and other times she went by herself for an exciting adventure as an unaccompanied minor flying to Puerto Rico.

Teens are trying to figure out who they are and who they want to become in a world that is very chaotic and uncertain.

Sofia Bella participated in many sports. Soccer and gymnastics were her passion. At recess, she was a fast, strong runner who preferred playing tag with boys and some other girls more than talking *"silly girl stuff,"* as she would call some of the conversations of her peers.

She had a gorgeous voice and a beautiful imagination that led her to have a passion for writing and musical theater. One of her Language Art teachers from the middle school said that Sofia was the best Juliette she's heard, when referring to Sofia reading Juliet from the *Romeo and Juliet* play by William Shakespeare.

Her creativity left behind many poems, drawings, paintings, and other projects, including Christmas ornaments honoring the birth of Jesus.

Why am I telling you all of this? I want you to know that no one is exempt from the effects of poor mental health, depression, isolation, suicidal ideation, or the hardships of going through adolescence. Teens are trying to figure out who they are and who they want to become in a world that is very chaotic and uncertain.

The Subject of Smart Phones

Sofia wanted a phone when she was 10 years old. *"Ma, all my friends have cell phones,"* she would argue. *"It is too early Sofia, you do not need one"*, I would say. We told her she needed to wait until she was at least 13 years old. She did not like the idea. Later, I came to realize that although most of her friends had cell phones, she was not the only one without a cell phone at age 12.

I remember a Father-Daughter dance in her school when she was a fifth grader. I was working as a volunteer. Part of the fun was having raffles for things the girls would like to have. Parents would buy tickets for the donated goods and the school made some money to support other activities. Steve bought Sofia 10 tickets for the raffle. Many things

Father–Daughter Dance at Saint Patrick's School, 2015

were being raffled off that night but she placed all of her tickets towards the raffle of a tablet. I was surprised to hear the master of the ceremony calling "*Sofia Wexler*" as the winner of a small tablet. She was beaming with joy. She did not have a cell phone but could now engage with friends on social media via the tablet, she thought. It took us a while to give her permission to use the tablet but we did. On her 13th birthday, she received her first iPhone. It was not the latest model but it was as dangerous as any smartphone at that tender age.

Letter to Mom by Sofia. April 2017 while a 6th grader

Dear mother, the tablet is very much cherished in my heart. Though thee may object my proposal to permit me to employ my electronic item, my acquaintance and I assure you that we will exploit superior decisions in the use of the device, thus not exasperating thee due to our boredom. Although I value thy permission for my associate to arrive at our residence, that does not keep monotony from successfully reaching us. We plead exceedingly for the permission of the use of the Galaxy Note Tablet 8.0. An only an affectionate mother would do so. I love you.

Sincerely,

Your beloved daughter Sofia

To this, I replied, "Sofia, my dear, do you know how much I love you?"

Tweenhood is especially hard in our times due to all the good, bad, and sometimes destructive information our kids have at their fingertips through their smartphones. A quick search on their phones leads them to ugly, even devastating, - "*This is how you deal with your unhappiness,*" "*This is how you look cool,*" "*This is how you get thin,*" "*This is how you fit in*" information in their tender minds that can ruin their lives forever.

Tweenhood is especially hard in our times due to all the good, bad, and sometimes destructive information our kids have at their fingertips through their smartphones.

Smartphones are complex electronics that can be very detrimental to our kids, especially the most vulnerable. Many parents say, *"But my kid is in so many extracurricular activities, he needs a phone to call me"* or *"I want to be able to call her."* I understand this need. I also want you to reflect on that need. Is it a real need or your desire to be able to contact your teen at any given time for your own sake? This is not a judgment but a call to dig deeper into the reasons why you feel the need to provide your pre-teen with a communication tool that is also a mini-computer. A smartphone is a window into a very disturbing world that will come to your teen whether they search for it or not. Artificial intelligence will find them, meet them through their screen, and provide all kinds of ideas and information without you even realizing it. Unfortunately, some of the ideas and information coming to them might not be in alignment with your values or what you want them to know at that early age. Think about this, your teen might be searching for comfy underwear and that could be a trigger to have a pop-up ad for porn. Sometimes, all it takes is a bit of curiosity to open one of those pop-ups to plug your teen into the disgusting world of pornography, sex trafficking via images, or worse. As easy as that.

Artificial intelligence will find them, meet them through their screen, and provide all kinds of ideas and information without you even realizing it.

When making your decision, also remember that their coach, teacher, and drama director have phones and they would be happy to lend their phone for a call. If you consider this to be intrusive, provide your kid with a dial phone without the smart part.

I am no expert in technology, but I've read some about the damage a smartphone can cause to a developing brain. Please know that brain development is not completed until about age 25.

Cell phones and their blue light can interfere with your kid's ability to fall asleep and concentrate for extended periods. It may also cause headaches, low memory, and poor attention to detail. I see so many babies with cell phones in their hands as a means of a pacifier. Many young parents are unaware of the damage it is causing to their little brains.

Please know that brain development is
not completed until about age 25.

As kids reach their teen years on their phones, they grow increasingly anxious wanting to know what are they missing or what is said about them. All of this drives them to be in a constant state of alert affecting their hormonal regulating system, interfering with brain development, and preventing much-needed restful time and social interaction with those around them. With a need to constantly check their social media accounts, teens are driving themselves to mental fatigue. This makes school work and functioning in general a very difficult task. Does this make more appealing the idea of having your teen call you from their coach's or teacher's phone when needed? I hope so.

Read more on the subject, don't take my word for it.

 Insight: If after all consideration, you are inclined to provide your teen with a smartphone, get informed on the possible effects on their development, monitor their use of social media, take note of their changes in behavior, and create boundaries and rules around the use of the phone. Agree upon where the phone will be stored overnight and what will be the consequences for misuse. After both parties agree, enforce the agreement! A phone is a privilege, not a necessity.

Also, invest in parental control apps or systems such as *Bark* to try to keep your child safe while navigating cyberspace. Your job is to protect them. When they are alone in their room with their smartphone, you can't protect them the same way.

Some schools are creating new policies to deal with the increasing use of smartphones during the school day and the disruption of learning that this creates. I know a couple of schools that had implemented lockable phone pouches to secure cell phones during the school day preventing distractions due to the use of social media and other apps. These pouches are lockable and are an alternative to keeping the phone in the student's hand instead of collecting phones before class as other schools do. An example of such a pouch is the *YONDR* security pouch.

Sofia (8 years old) was carefree and loved to play with water.

It is All a Balancing Act

Now that you have grasped the reality of how hard it is to be a teen in today's age, add challenging circumstances at home on top of their normal adolescent pains. You now have a potentially lethal combination of facts and circumstances that can lead to alcoholism, drug addiction, physical abuse, self-harm, or suicide. All of these actions, intended by the teen to cope with the situation at hand, end up trapping them in a vicious cycle that is hard to break and, in most cases, is self-destructive. They don't realize how deep in trouble they are until it is getting out of hand. At that point, they don't know how or want to ask for help and try to deal with the situation on their own, something that they are not qualified or prepared to do.

Asking for help is hard for anyone.

If this happened to my beloved Sofia Bella, it can happen to a teen you know regardless of their background and circumstances. Teens try to keep things inside. They will not tell you what is wrong in their lives, much less ask for help. Asking for help is not for them. They think they are beyond that and should figure things out by themselves.

Let's admit it, asking for help is hard for anyone. We don't want to be considered weak or foolish. We want to believe that we are smart and self-reliant. It is the same for teens. They are at a point in their development where they are questioning authority, finding new ideas, and different ways of doing things while forming their judgments. Many times, right or wrong, their conclusions and judgments contradict what they learned from parents, teachers, and other authority figures. Hopefully, by this time, you have a strong relationship with your teen, and they will bring forward their discoveries trying to understand why they don't match with what they learned from you. Your teen should be able to respectfully confront you, explain their point of view, and hear your side as well.

We want to believe that we are smart and
self-reliant. It is the same for teens.

The path just described although ideal, in many cases will not happen. Many times, the teen will confront parents/caregivers during an argument when things are heated and will simply distrust whatever the parents have to say. They will stop bringing forward questions or contradictions they find. They will search for answers themselves and check with peers if they perceive that the adult is not open to a fair and respectful exchange of ideas.

Consider that the conclusions and ideas they start formulating about the world around them are not bad or ill-intended. Indeed, they are a reflection of a person who is maturing and developing. One thing that our teens need to know and understand at this stage of their development is that their life experiences and knowledge are limited. This limitation can lead them to assume positions or start unfounded arguments just to be in opposition to authority and feel that their voice is heard. What they can do instead is to bring their ideas and questions forward with a curious mind to learn from others with different experiences and points of view. This is very hard to do, even for adults.

Teens can benefit from having the humility and maturity to validate their ideas and conclusions with an adult they respect and who has an open mind. Be that adult to the teens around you.

Caregivers need to be able to recognize when they are wrong and change their point of view accordingly without the fear of losing authority.

On the other hand, parents and caregivers need to show that we care by listening without judging or cutting them off assuming we know what they are going to say. Adults need to be patient as they try to understand their teen's point of view. Most importantly, caregivers need to be able to recognize when they are wrong and change their point of view accordingly without the fear of losing authority. Sometimes we avoid reversing course to save face thinking we will look weak and unimportant. Nothing can be further from the truth. We gain more respect from our teens when we can admit we were wrong and explain to our teens why we had the position we held before.

Remember that failing is part of the growing process.

In conclusion, going through adolescence is hard. There could be personal circumstances that make it harder, and teens will not share this information freely. Teens will try to solve things themselves, and they should as part of their development to become fully functioning reliable adults. Unfortunately, this means that they may not check in with a trusted adult when the issue or problem could use adult discernment. When approaching teens, do it with compassion, and ask questions to better understand without judgment. This was something hard for me and I am still working on it. Our preconceived notions and personal judgments of what is good or bad can get in the way when dealing with our teens. We want to teach and protect them but instead, our judgment can push them farther away from us. Put yourselves in their place. Challenge their views with love and respect knowing that they are doing the best they can with the knowledge and experience they have. Remember that failing is part of the growing process. Let them fail and encourage them to talk openly with you as part of the learning process when they do. We are not perfect! Neither are our teens.

 Insight: If you have a teen or work with a teen at school, camp, church, or in any other scenario, please keep reading. The next chapters will provide words of encouragement for you, ideas, resources, and a group of Sofia Bella's writings so you can get to know her soul a little better and hopefully find ways to connect with the teens in your life or those that you serve.

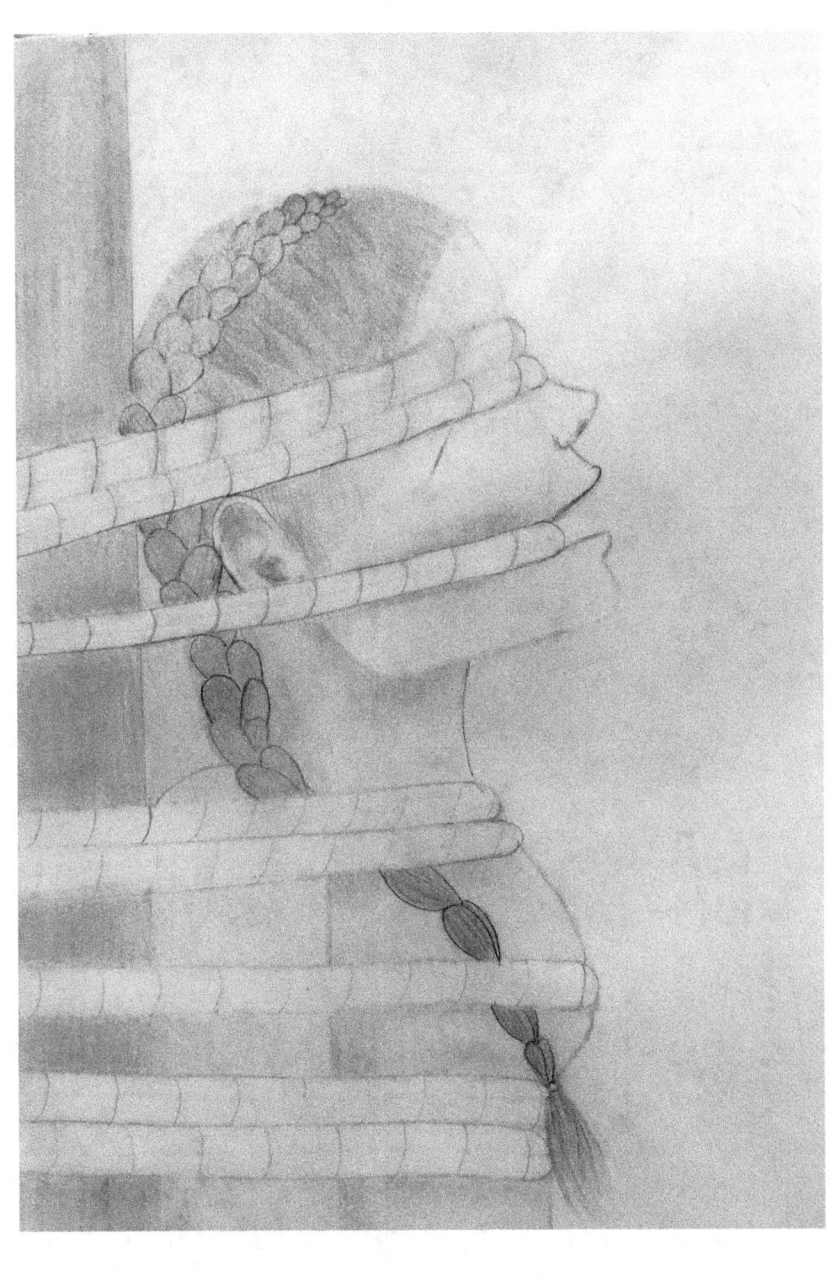

A Poem by Sofia Bella Wexler

No title or date (estimated to be written around freshman year)

I don't have the energy

For anything

Anymore

I wish I could

Shut the door,

Curl up on the floor,

And cry 'bout how much I abhor

Myself.

I wish one day

I could wake up and say

That I love me,

But I don't, see;

I hate my life,

Hate how everyone lies

How I am stuck in this

Nightmare

They say "life is a dream"

Well, then, come and wake me

'cause I don't want to be

In this world full of fear.

I don't want to be here.

Where the blood of the innocents

Smeared every minute and

I just want this to end.

I just want to forget

I wish I was never born

I know people will mourn

But they'll move on

They'll sing life's song

And I hope in every measure

They will find a bit of pleasure.

I just couldn't find mine.

CHAPTER 3

How Can I Help

Parents of Teens

Parenting is hard work. When kids arrive into their teen years, they could be pretty self-sufficient imposing less mental and physical work on us. With this change comes a bit of freedom for parents who can now take care of individual needs or work a little harder toward their personal or professional goals. This is all good and very possible. The caution here is to keep your eyes wide open and your intuition sharp to identify when your kids will require greater attention.

During this age, teens may need you the most only at a different level. Trying to be their friend or giving them total independence may seem like a good idea. Consider the possibility that they may not be ready for that. You are still the parent! You will need to make tough and unpopular decisions, enforce rules, and administer consequences. It is a delicate balance between not suffocating and not letting go completely. As much as possible, let them make their own decisions. They will fail sometimes and that is part of the process, as I previously said. Don't rescue them but hold them accountable so they can learn valuable lessons. This is what they need from you. You can be best friends later. For now, be a parent first and a friendly trusted adult second.

This is what they need from you. You can be best friends later.
For now, be a parent first and a friendly trusted adult second.

Support your teen with love, patience, understanding, and many prayers. Condemnation and telling them to *"get your act together"* will not help and can make things worse. Find little signs of progress and praise your teen. Progress could be picking up after themselves or thanking someone for something they receive. These two examples require positive energy and self-awareness, which signals great progress.

The heavier the restrictions, the more rebellion.

Be aware that the heavier the restrictions, the more rebellion. Research on parenting style has indicated that parents on the very lenient, "hands-off" end of the spectrum AND those on the stringent, rigid, or controlling end of the spectrum tend to have more disciplinary issues with their children. Those who listen, respect, stay aware, work on connection, and allow mutual decision-making have a greater chance of raising children with good decision-making skills, fewer behavioral issues, and more respect. Keep a cool head. If you keep it together and respect them, you will eventually earn their respect back and, possibly in the future, their understanding.

Our reaction to what happens or what is said by our
teens speaks louder than any words we can say.

As the Greek philosopher Epictetus said; *"It's not what happens to you, but how you react to it that matters."* In any given situation, our reaction to what happens or what is said by our teens speaks louder than any words we can say. When we approach the event hysterically and with rage, they will not hear *"I love you, care for you, and want to help you grow"* but they will hear *"I can't believe you are doing/saying that again, I told you many times! When will you learn?"* Expressions like this generate self-doubt and make them feel inadequate, undermining confidence and self-esteem. Guarding our reaction is a big challenge. I struggle with this too, ask my older daughter. With time, I've learned to be more self-aware. You can moderate your reactions and control the words that come out of your mouth. You can do this by not giving in to the strong feelings of the moment. The parenting style I used with my older daughter when I was a younger and less experienced mother is very different than the parenting style, I am using with Daniel today. I hope my oldest daughter can understand this one day and forgive my mistakes.

Be mindful, respectful, and strategic about rules and consequences. Always remind your teens that you love them, especially when you are mad or disappointed. They act as if they don't care if you love them, BUT THEY DO. They need to hear about your unconditional love and care often. Declare your love and care both away from the moments of tension as well as in the middle of a heated argument.

Teens can't help themselves. They don't even know what is happening to them. It is all very confusing. Asking them to figure out how to get better or make better choices can only increase their feelings of worthlessness and inability to function. It can also cause more anxiety. Read about adolescents and mental health so that you can try to understand what is going on. There are resources at the end of this book to start you on that journey.

I know it is frustrating, and at times it feels hopeless. Please find someone who can help you navigate options - don't endure this alone. I know of parents who are so embarrassed that they prefer to pretend that all is well or go through the storm alone. Please don't do this to yourself. You are not the only one dealing with these types of situations. After Sofia's death and my openness to talk about the subject, I had parents approach me with their heartaches. People that I would never suspect having issues with their teens or young adults shared their troubles with me. You need someone that will be your ally in searching for answers and alternatives as well as helping you think through things. Find a friend or a professional who is detached from the emotions and pains of the situation.

It may also be that your teen needs a counselor. Try exploring resources at school or within the community that can help your teen or both of you.

But I am Not a Parent of a Teen

If you work with teens, thank you for taking on this work of love. You are in the middle of the action. You have a front-row seat to the day-in and day-out drama in the lives of these amazing young people away from home. You may feel that you do not want to intrude or that you do not have the authority, but you have a very important role as both an observer and reporter. Do not dismiss their behaviors or lack of engagement at times as just something normal for their age. There might be a storm brewing inside, and you could be the only one who can notice subtle changes or clues.

As an outsider, you might have more access to the real truth in their lives than a person with authority over them, as they will not have to worry about disappointing you or hurting you.

A teen in distress is waiting for someone to be interested enough to ask a question so that they can start revealing what is in their minds and hearts. As an outsider, you might have more access to the real truth in their lives than a person with authority over them, as they will not have to worry about disappointing you or hurting you. After all, you are just a teacher, coach, camp counselor, or insert your title. Don't expect that they will open up right away. They need you, but they do not know they do. They might be dismissive at first to see if you are really interested. Be respectful. Keep an appropriate distance and re-engage when you have the opportunity. They need to trust you before they go deep with you. As with any other person, no matter the age, having some level of relationship or sharing a common interest always makes conversations easier to have.

My suggestion to you is to read through this book, get some insights into a stormy mind who might need your approach, check out the resources provided, learn more about mental illness/suicidal ideation, and figure out what the procedures are at your school or workplace to deal with a teen who is in distress or having suicidal thoughts. Maybe your impulse would be to alert the parents, and that might be the right thing to do. FIRST, consider evaluating if the source of the conflict, anxiety, depression, or suicidal thoughts is coming from someone or something at home before you contact their mom/dad/caregiver. YOU COULD SAVE A LIFE.

The following verbatim is something you can say to a young person in distress. Read it many times, change it, make it your own, and use it often.

> *"I want you to know without the shadow of a doubt that life is messy but worth living. Behind that dark cloud that troubles your soul, the sun shines brightly and purifies every dark thought, making it all bright and beautiful again. Let's find a way to ease your anxiety and learn how to overcome the moments of desperation. When you are in distress, call 988 or someone you trust to keep you safe and wait for the dark cloud to pass. When you are safe, recognize that you may need more help than you think to avoid having that cloud become powerful and overwhelming to the point of no return. YOU ARE WORTH SAVING! I want to help because I care for you."*

About Counselors, Social Workers, and Such

These are professionals with degrees in human development and behavioral sciences who are making a difference by helping others develop a healthy way to cope with life. Those are the coaches you want to have on the bench with you. They will help you learn different ways to better engage your teen and manage your fears and anxieties. They can also help your teen to better understand what is happening to them. These individuals can direct you early in the process towards resources that you can explore and have in your toolbox before you need them. Early interventions can make a difference.

> *Not all mental health professionals are created equal. If your teen is not opening up truthfully to her counselor, you must change to another professional.*

On the topic of counselors and mental healthcare professionals for your teen, one thing I learned and want to pass on to you is that not all mental health professionals are created equal. If your teen is not opening up truthfully to her counselor, you must change to another professional.

Finding a mental health care professional who works for your family is not an easy task. You need to find what works best for your teen and this could take visiting more than one. You will encounter barriers such as a limited number of professionals available in your area who work with teens. Also, your insurance, type of coverage, or lack of insurance can limit your options. This last one was a struggle for us. Keep searching. There is always a way. Know that in our case, COVID-19 made everything twice as difficult but it could be much better for you.

Be aware that there is a difference between patient-counselor confidentiality or privacy for the patient and knowing how things are going. I was told by Sofia Bella's therapist that she could not share their conversations with me, which I understood. What I failed to do was to follow up more closely with the counselor regarding how Sofia was progressing and if the counselor was successful in connecting with her.

I also didn't realize that I could share information with the counselor from my perspective, even if the counselor could not reciprocate and share specifics about my teen with me. The counselor could have listened to my concerns without breaking confidentiality. Also, I needed to ask more general questions to better understand how much progress was made in between sessions. I made sure Sofia Bella was on her remote sessions and trusted that the process would work and things would be resolved with time. I was naïve. I missed figuring out early enough that my teen needed a change of pace or a different person. It was after Sofia Bella was gone that I realized how little was accomplished during her private sessions due to Sofia's lack of participation or desire to get better.

If your teen is making excuses, missing therapy, or ending therapy earlier, it is time to dig deeper into why this is happening. Maybe she is not comfortable with the therapist or maybe the therapist is not a good match for your teen's personality or particular situation. A change of strategy, therapist, or therapeutic orientation can make a big difference.

When hospital stays started, we were assigned to different counselors and psychiatrists for follow-ups. This was in addition to Sofia's primary private psychologist. We were under COVID-19 protocols, the availability of resources was limited, and follow-ups were via virtual technology. She needed face-to-face therapy. At times I felt as if I was running from one place to another with Sofia in my arms trying to find help when nothing seemed to work. She was "bleeding" out her life and no one knew how to stop it. I was losing her a little bit at a time. Looking back, it seems as if there was a lot of activity with little result.

I can see now more clearly the fact that Sofia Bella was sicker than we thought she was and what she led us to believe. She did not want to be helped or she was in such a dark place that she could not see how others could help her situation. She chose to isolate even more.

Before moving to the next topic, I want to pause and elevate a prayer for the minds and hearts of teens in distress right at this moment and for the counselors who treat them. Pray with me.

> *"Lord Jesus, you are the light of the world. May the light of your merciful love penetrate the dark areas of the minds of those struggling with depression right now. Help them to find a way to open their door to the possibility of fighting their distress, anxieties, and depression through the help of others, especially their mental health providers. In Jesus' precious name, we pray. Amen"*

Drop the Mask

Do not be ashamed! When you are caring for a teen with suicidal ideation or other mental health challenges, you must know that it is not your fault. Maybe you feel you could have done something differently and maybe there is some truth to that. But at this time things are more complicated and just a parenting style change will not be enough.

This is also NOT the time to look for someone to blame. If you believe that God is a God of love and mercy, hopefully, you will realize that this is not a punishment from God either. This is not happening to punish your child, yourself, or your family. You need God's love and merciful heart to go through this, embrace Him in prayer. Don't blame God, yourself, or anyone else. You will only grow bitter and waste precious time.

Many parents are going through the same trials. When I was going through my trials, I talked with anyone willing to listen. I asked for their prayers and ideas on how to tackle what was going on. I also activated many prayer warriors to pray for the restoration of health and peace for

Sofia. I prayed for her every day and with her when she would let me.

Do what you feel you need to do without shame and without asking for permission. Hiding behind the image of a perfect family can oftentimes only make things harder for you, your teen, and everyone involved. Besides, wearing a mask can be exhausting and you need all your energy and clarity of mind you can have to support your teen.

Spring into action! It is your child we are talking about. I am rooting and praying for you! Things could end up better than expected. In the worst case, like mine, you will be left with the peace that comes when you know you gave it your all and fought fearlessly.

I have said this before and will say it again as I leave you with more of Sofia Bella's work: This is not a matter of who is right and who is wrong. It is a matter of understanding what your teen needs, becoming humble, dropping your ego, and reaching out to understand and connect.

What they feel in a moment of desperation when they want to end their lives lasts for only a short time, which will seem like an eternity for them, and it will pass.

Each teen is precious, unique, and irreplaceable. God gave them a precious soul at conception, and they have a specific mission to accomplish in this world with their God-given talents. What they feel in a moment of desperation when they want to end their lives lasts for only a short time, which will seem like an eternity for them, and it will pass. Believe me, they do not want to end their lives every hour of their day. One day they could be very happy and you might think that things are getting better, and then the next day they might be a total mess. I experienced that with my angel. It is an exhausting emotional rollercoaster that takes a toll on everyone around.

The *"I can't stand the pain any longer"* or *'they will be better if I am dead'* thoughts come in a moment of despair. In those moments teens are scared and afraid of what they are thinking. Be the hand that leads them to a better understanding of their sickness. If you can't, find someone who can help. You need to find ways to crack open the door to their inner dark room. I know it is scary, but you have to try. They start closing up, little by little, like a flower that withers slowly after they bloom. With a closed door, closed mind, and closed heart, no one will be able to help them. At this point, they can't seem to find the will to open the door to the possibility of a healthier way. In the end, and without help, they believe their sick brain and lose the battle to mental illness and suicidal ideation, leaving behind many broken hearts. They find a permanent solution to a passing moment of distress and agony – SUICIDE.

*Be the hand that leads them to a better
understanding of their sickness.*

This is a sickness that in most cases can be fixed or at the very least managed. Teens can survive mental health illness in the majority of the cases. Your teen was entrusted to you, and there is a reason why they are in your life. God has a specific plan for them, and you are the chosen one to guide them with charity and love. You got this!

Your job is to let them know that other teens are going through the same struggles, that there are people and healthcare professionals ready and eager to help, and that people around them are waiting for them to cross these turbulent waters, embrace life with all its highs and lows, and make a difference in this world.

There is Hope!

Good news! Not all troubled young people with suicidal ideation end up taking their lives. More cases than not they end up living productive lives, some with struggles but still making a

Drawing of a girl, 7th grade.

difference in the lives of those around them. For example, consider the case of Susan Rose Blauner. She figured out, with help, what was going on in her brain, opened herself to receiving help, and had the willingness to stay alive by engaging in therapy. She wrote a book that I found in my public library, *How I Stayed Alive When My Brain Was Trying to Kill Me - One Person's Guide to Suicide Prevention.*

When I started reading the book, I was angry at myself. Why didn't I do this search earlier in the process? Would this be a resource that she could relate to? Would this book have made any difference in how she approached her sickness and therapy? I don't know. But I know I discovered it for a reason. That reason is to share it with you so that you don't have the same questions I do.

Here is a quote from page 43: "*To experience lasting relief, we have to be willing to keep ourselves physically safe long enough to be able to learn and practice new skills while we let go of old behaviors and thought patterns.*" Susan Rose shares with her audience that "*Everything depression tells you is a lie.*"

This book can make a difference for your teen. Suicidal ideation can be battled. Your teen can survive it. It can be done. She did it! Praise and thank you, Jesus!

There are also those whose suicide attempts take them to a path of redemption, self-care, and a zest for life after looking death in the eye through a suicide attempt that did not keep them from living. Some brave ones go on to build ministries and make it their life's mission to help others who are in the same desperate situation they once were. Beautiful Kristen Jane Anderson and her Reaching You Ministries is an example of this beautiful transformation. Her book *Life in Spite of Me – Extraordinary Hope After a Fatal Choice* tells her story and how she turned around to live a fuller, rich, God-filled life. Maybe there is something there that can spark a flame of hope in your teen's heart.

Can I Speak to Your Teen?

I get it! Living is hard and being a teenager sometimes sucks.

Most adults, when looking back at their lives, realize that the years of being a teen were the best years of their life. They just did not know it at

the time. This can also be true for you. With that in mind, I encourage you to reach out when you feel overwhelmed or in need of answers. If it is too hard to reach out or you do not know how to or whom to, **call the 988 Lifeline for Suicide Prevention**. It is an easy number to remember! The 988 line provides emotional support for people in suicidal crisis or emotional distress. The line is available 24/7, it is free and confidential, with support in English and Spanish. Even if you are not sure if the service is for you, CALL THEM! and let them figure it out. You do not need to figure it out alone and they will not get mad if you call many times as long as you need their support.

Call the 988 Lifeline for Suicide Prevention.

You can also try letting in someone who has been knocking at your door. Accept their help for your pain as long as it is a healthy alternative.

Drugs, alcohol, and other unhealthy ways will make your pain worse in the end. Do you remember when you were younger and would put up a fight to avoid taking that horrible medicine for your cough or fever? When you grew older, you realized that the medicine tasted bad but made you better and got you out playing with your friends sooner. When you understood this concept, you finally stopped fighting the medicine. In the same way, stop fighting yourself and avoiding speaking with someone. With the right person, your fears and anxiety can only get better. Find a counselor that you can work with. If that counselor does not work for you, it is perfectly fine and encouraged that you change it. Keep trying. Your life depends on it.

Most probably you have a friend trying to help you. Someone who knows the real you, the you that you would rather hide from others when you pretend that everything is okay. This friend stays with you on the phone for long hours or leaves a chat open on your favorite application so you can feel that there is someone with you at all times. Your friend, like some of Sofia Bella's friends, is trying their best to do something that they are not prepared to do. They are desperately trying to save you while keeping your friendship because they care. They are scared!

Your friends do not have all the answers. They know something is not right. They are probably frustrated with you and tired of you not following their suggestions. They feel as if you are not trying hard enough when the truth is that you might be at the end of your rope with no energy or desire to try anymore. You might be thinking that it is best for all if you just let go of yourself. Nothing is farther from reality. Giving up is harder on everyone you love and want to protect from your pain — especially your friends.

Keeping things in secret is a dangerous proposition and one that can haunt your friends for life.

Your friends do not want to betray your trust. They love you! At the same time, they might want to contact an adult. They are encouraged, by all of us working to prevent suicide, to find a trusted adult with whom to share their worries for you. DO NOT get mad at them. It is not a betrayal. It is a desperate attempt to save you from yourself. Keeping things in secret is a dangerous proposition and one that can haunt your friends for life. You do not want them to live with that guilt for the rest of their lives. Let them get help for you. Love them and know that those who look for trusted adults to work with your situation care for you and want to be by your side. They want you alive and healthy.

Let me share something with you. My daughter, Sofia Bella, was funny, artistic, passionate, smart, loved animals, and had a very generous heart. She could console the saddest person with her very sensitive soul and could make someone laugh on their worst rainy day. Don't take it from me- I am just her mom. Take it from the many notes of gratitude left at her funeral by friends and those her life touched. I've included a few at the end of this chapter for you to read.

Imagine how the lives of those around her could still be impacted if she was able to spread more of that love for many years to come. How many lives could have been changed and laughter shared? The way the world misses Sofia Bella's existence, her talents, and her work is the same way that the world around you will miss you if you are gone.

*Suicide is a permanent solution to a
possibly temporary situation.*

And don't you dare say to me or in your mind that the world will not care if you are gone. That is a lie that is growing in your very ill brain. It is not the reality of your life or the lives of those around you. YOU WILL BE MISSED TREMENDOUSLY. Please stay.

Finally, when you have a chance search on YouTube for a video/poem called *The Morning After I Killed Myself.* It is a reflective piece written by Meggie Royer that pretends to go into the mind of a soul that died by suicide and how it could feel the morning after. It is a message about the finality of suicide, the impact it has on loved ones, and the lost opportunity for another day. Suicide is a permanent solution to a possibly temporary situation. My favorite version is a video made/produced by *illneas*, uploaded on November 29, 2020.

Picture taken by Maria Martina in her garden. Summer 2021.

Notes of Gratitude for Sofia Bella's Life Left at Her Funeral Mass

"To my favorite. My little pony fan, professional pancake maker, guitarist, soccer player, artist, sister, and best friend. I will truly miss our sleepovers where we would laugh all night, and you would let me curl your hair and paint your nails. I am so thankful for you."
CZARLIZE

"Sofia was and is one of the most pure-hearted, loving, witty, and truly good people I have ever known. She never had a negative word to say about another person. Her understanding of the people and world around her was astute beyond her years, but even more impressive was her humility and undying generosity. I think of her daily."
ANA

"Bella loved art. We were in theater class together. ... I will never forget her endless creativity and imagination."
KELSEY

"I partnered with her for one English project. We wrote a story together about a horse. She was an amazing writer and I think about her every English class."
ANONYMOUS

"I met Bella in October 2020. Although we had never met in person before, she made me feel like we had known each other for years. ...The best moment from that night is when four of us carried Bella above our heads through the corn (maze)."
DAVID

"… my favorite memory of her would be when she was one of the first to climb the rock wall. From then on, I saw her as a strong and brave girl. Even I couldn't do it (climbing the rock wall). I wish I had gotten to meet her well."
LEONEL

"In gym, she would swing upside down on the climbing ropes and just laugh hysterically. Her laugh was my favorite sound."
ANONYMOUS

"I'll miss your hugs."
BELLA G.

"…she (Sofia Bella) was the only one who knew the real me. I love her so much and it hurts that I won't see her again or talk to her."
DAISY

"I always wished to know Bella better. She was a beautiful girl who was a wonderful friend to many people. I wished she knew how much she was loved and will be missed."
ANONYMOUS

PART TWO

Our Story – Our Battle

CHAPTER 4

The Age of Innocence: In Her
Own Words ... and Mine

In the following chapters, you will find the bulk of Sofia Bella's writings through the years. She loved the written word and was an avid reader. Reading and writing were a window to different worlds for her, and she loved to explore them all.

The excerpts I chose to share with you include at times my commentary and observations of what was going on at the time. It is my hope that through reading both you can get into Sofia Bella's world from both perspectives, hers and mine, and start finding similarities or differences that help you better understand your teen's world and perspective as well as your own struggle.

Kids are innocent little people with big imaginations, bigger hearts, and much creativity. If we search carefully, we will be able to find that creative, happy little person inside our teens. Once we connect with that little person, we will see our troubled teen in a different light and with more compassion.

"When I was a child, I spoke like a child, I thought like a child, I reasoned like a child..."

1 COR. 13:11 (NEW REVISED STANDARD VERSION)

Daddy's little girl.

A Sensible Soul. A Curious Mind.

There was nothing Steve and I wanted more after getting married in September of 2004 than having a child together. It was also God's plan since I got pregnant only after a month of our wedding. I realized I was pregnant in November 2004 and held the news from Steve until Christmas that year. I shared the news with my daughter, though. She was 11 years old and I wanted her to be part of the excitement and Christmas surprise for Steve. She was so happy with the news and was very good at keeping the secret.

On Christmas morning, I gave Steve a very special Christmas gift. It was a composite of three of our favorite wedding photos in a rectangular frame. Steve smiled and said, "*So cute, thank you!*" I said, "*Open the photo frame on the back*". He probably thought, "*What a strange request*", yet, he complied. He found a folded paper. "*Labs?*", he asked. He had no clue. I said, "*Read!*" He was puzzled. It took a bit but finally, he said "*We are having a baby!*". I screamed, "*YES!*" We hugged and my daughter ran to us. Everyone in the family was overwhelmed and excited about the news of this little bundle of joy already growing in my belly.

Sofia Bella was born at 8:19 AM on 8/19/2005. She made a big entrance with the most beautiful eyelashes and the prettiest little angelic face that I've ever seen. Even the nurses were astonished by her cuteness and big lashes. She was a perfect angel sent to us by God. I knew then she was special, and she distinguished herself from all the babies in the hospital nursery with her calm demeanor. I bet all the moms delivering that day thought the same of their babies, but Sofia Bella was something special in my eyes.

"Heaven is a special place because it is Holy and in it is Christ the Lord. You can see God and Jesus. You can live in Heaven forever and you can see all the Saints." (6 years old)

Drawing by Sofia Bella. Second Grade.

Between our faith formation at home and her catholic school, Sofia developed great love and devotion for Jesus, Mary, and the Saints. She wanted to know more about Heaven since she was a little girl.

Sofia Bella was a very sensitive little girl. People would describe her as shy but when she was with her friends, she was outgoing, silly, and had a very loud laugh. You would never guess how outgoing she could be. She always had this mysterious and angelic smile that would melt any heart and get her out of any trouble.

At Six Flags - Great America with Natalia on her left and Ainsley, Summer 2019.

"I love Six Flags. The Wizard is my favorite ride because it is scary." (6 years old)

Sofia was fierce and brave. She was not intimidated by frogs, lizards, or heights like other girls her age. Spiders were another thing; she was scared of them. She also loved to climb tall trees. Not afraid of the dark either, as a teen, she loved riding intense rollercoasters at Six Flags Great America, especially at night time. Her sense of adventure and curiosity is greatly missed.

"My favorite animal is a panda bear because they are cute, and funny, and cuddly, and friendly." (6 years old)

Sofia Bella was funny, friendly, and I would say very cute. I guess that is why she liked pandas so much, they were so similar to her in cuteness and lovability. She left behind a pair of panda slippers that I use every so often when I want to be "in her shoes" remembering the things she loved.

If you do this, you will live a perfect life.

Jesus first. Others second. Yourself last. (7 years old)

No words for this one. It explains itself and gives testament to her faith and her love for humanity.

She loved nature. Below are some beautiful expressions of her love of nature.

April is rain. April is showers.

April is filling the world with all kinds of flowers.

April is bursting. April is blooming.

April is when all the green starts resuming. (7 years old)

Sofia's hand holding a bouquet of wildflowers collected during a road trip in June 2020.

May is inspiring! Can you believe it? It is the hottest month of the year (so far). I love May! Flowers! Rainbows! Butterflies! Birds! All these beautiful things. I love it! I love God! I love the world! (7 years old)

I Love

I love too many things! Chocolate, family, friends, books, report cards, vacations, tiny baby unicorns with little bity horns, ice cream, blankets, pillows, shakes, shoes, pancakes, movies, waffles, stuff animals, braces, jewelry, and clothes. (8 years old)

Letter to the Holy Spirit

Dear Holy Spirit,

Give me kindness, love, peace, joy, goodness, patience, gentleness, faithfulness and self-control. All of those things help me through life. If I participate in the fruits of the Holy Spirit, things will go easy. Help me follow God's example. Jesus sacrificed his life for us. All of us. If he did something for us, we should do something for him.

Amen. (9 years old)

Her favorite thing to do was riding horses. Summer 2013.

No Title

I once owned a horse named Lield.

She loved to go graze in the field

She neighed with pride,

She triumphed with stride,

When I tried to squeeze through

She would yield. (9 years old)

"My favorite season is winter because it is fun. You get to make a snowman, make snow angels, and throw snowballs. It is just lots of fun!" (9 years old)

Sofia loved playing in the snow and making snow angels. I remember a big snowfall when she was about nine years old and Daniel was four. She wanted so badly to go out and play in the snow. Little Daniel wanted to follow his sister. The snow was too deep for little Daniel. We sat Daniel on a sled and she pulled him through the snow just like Dad would do to her when she was younger. She felt so big helping Daniel and doing something Dad would do for her. They had so much fun! I enjoyed through the window taking pictures and creating a visual memory of that happy special time when she was a big sister playing and caring for her baby brother. Life was good. I was grateful to God for the blessing of two additional kids, even though I only asked for one more. God is funny and wise like that.

―――――――――――――――

I was grateful to God for the blessing of two additional kids, even though I only asked for one more. God is funny and wise like that.

―――――――――――――――

Insight: Talking about snow, Sofia's biggest theater role was as Olaf in the musical Frozen at Warren Township High School. My favorite line in the musical was, "There are people that are worth melting for." When she said that line, my heart melted. She would melt for any of her friends if that meant helping them or making them happy. It is winter as I write these lines. I bet she is making many beautiful snow angels in Heaven.

In fifth grade, she was one of the angels in a legion of angels during that year's Saint Patrick Catholic School Christmas program. She did not want the play to end. Sofia enjoyed every rehearsal. She loved being an angel and all the singing that went with the role. She told me that it made her feel special transporting her to a magical place. What could be more magical and amazing than the birth of Jesus in Bethlehem and a legion of Angels announcing his birth?

Sofia was not happy when she learned that as a 6th grader, she could not do it again because it was a 5th-grader thing. She kept her golden angel halo and used it to decorate her room during Christmas for a couple of years as a remembrance of that special time. That angelic participation touched her soul deeply. When I remember this, I think about how happy she must be now hearing angelic music forever in the Kingdom of our Heavenly Father. When I see clouds forming figures in the sky, I always try to find angels. When I do, I imagine it is her making cloud angels to say hi. My heart rejoices with that thought.

"My favorite Holiday is Christmas because you get whatever you want. It is like being a Queen or King." (9 years old)

Her innocence at this time in her life (9 years/old) was beautiful. I enjoyed and facilitated every one of her Christmases to make sure they were magical and that Jesus was at the center of each one. I remember that when she would want something relatively expensive for Christmas, I would say *"That is a very expensive gift sweetie, I am not sure about you getting that."* Sometimes it was not that expensive, but I wanted her to appreciate the value of money. She would reply, *"Don't worry ma', I will ask Santa, I know he can."*

This reminds me of the year that she was eager to have Caroline, an American Girl doll that represented a historical character from 1812 in the United States. We already had an American Girl (AG) doll in the house that belonged to her sister but she was in love with Caroline and her story. I tried to steer her away from wanting another AG doll in the house but my strategy did not work. She kept saying that Santa was going to take care of it and that I should not have to worry about it.

As Christmas got closer, I realized that she was convinced that Santa was going to bring Caroline home for her. I was in trouble. I began searching for the best price available to make her dream come true and keep Santa alive. Trust me, there are no good deals when it comes to American Girl dolls, especially if it is close to Christmas and you need them to ship it faster than usual. It was all worth it, though. It made my momma's heart so happy when on Christmas morning Sofia's eyes light up as she hugged her new friend Caroline. She looked at me and said, *"I told you ma'!"* I took a picture of both of my girls with their own AG dolls as a reminder of that special Christmas morning.

The following year she wanted a horse and stable for Caroline. She got them. Not from the American Girl store but a Target version. She was happy, nonetheless. Sofia Bella was humble and down to earth with no preferences for specific brands, even when she was in high school. She was very mindful of money and hated wasting money on unnecessary things.

I remember one afternoon at the beginning of her junior year; she received about 5 different little packages from an online store. She looked at me confidently and proudly said, *"Don't worry ma'. I am not wasting all my money. All of this is for under twenty dollars or so."* She was working at Culver's at the time, feeling independent, browsing and buying little things for herself. I was so proud of my beautiful teen.

Never wasteful and always thrifty, she was good at recycling things or getting things at a second-hand store. Sofia loved to take care of the environment.

A funny story about Sofia has to do with how much she loved the environment. She hated seeing garbage left everywhere. From an early age, she was always picking up garbage when we were walking around the neighborhood, hiking, or after a public event like a parade. She could not understand why people would throw garbage without any care. Against our advice to avoid picking up garbage without gloves, she would always show up to the car with her hands full of trash asking where she could find the closest garbage can. She continued this practice into her high school years.

"My dad makes me smile. My dad likes to work very hard. He likes to break things apart and put them back together." *(10 years old)*

Sofia Bella had her dad's sense of humor and funny attitude towards things. Later, she enjoyed learning things with him and working on projects around the house. She loved learning how things worked, and her dad loved explaining and taking the time to teach her how to fix or build things. Steve remembers those days with tenderness.

"I can be a friend by ...being respectful, caring for one another, helping each other, doing stuff for them. That's what is all about it!" *(8 years old)*

She was a good friend, loyal to those she loved and always wanting to make them laugh. She met her two best friends when she was only three years old. It was perfect as they were our neighbors across the street and their parents became like a second mom and dad to Sofia Bella.

These three girls were inseparable. They loved playing together. As they grew older, they started the ASC club in our basement. ASC stood for Arriana, Sofia, and Czarlize. The ASC Club was a place to let their imagination and creativity run wild. It was very well organized with rules for their members and fancy stationery that they created. The girls were 8, 7, and 6 years old when their club was well established. It lasted for years. Each of its three members had their own "desk" where they made their art projects such as cards, book markers, and many other things. A "No Boys Allowed" rule came into place as Sofia's brother got older and wanted to be a member. Decorated with pictures and encouraging messages, the club also did some community work. Once they made a lot of bracelets to send some joy to kids in Peru through the Saint Patrick Church in Wadsworth Peru Mission ministry.

From left to right: Czarlize, Sofia, Arriana during the summer of 2021.

In addition to her ASC friends, Sofia also had three best friends from grade school. These three friends were together since kindergarten and through 8th grade graduation. Natalia, Ainsley, Marie, and Sofia learned and prayed together, helped each other on school projects, and enjoyed many school activities, birthday parties, and sleepovers. They were a quartet of school friends. Each one was beautifully different. Together they created beautiful notes of long-lasting friendship.

I remember when Sofia dragged Natalia to cheerleading practices in eighth grade. Natalia wanted to make Sofifi, as she called her, happy and went along with her. I think Natalia only cheered for one of the games. She wanted to be with Sofia but also had other commitments. Sofia and Natalia spent weekends together at the Steubenville Youth Catholic Conference on two different occasions. They stayed at a dorm on the campus where the conference was held. They were like sisters. They stayed awake until late talking about their lives and dreams. Here is a note that Natalia left at Sofia's funeral.

Natalia and Sofia during Confirmation April 2019.

"I remember when Sofifi and I went to Steubenville together for the first time in 7ᵗʰ grade and we had so much fun. We stayed super late just talking and we got to share a room so it was just like a sleepover. I remember when we went to Adoration and to the music concert (worship music). We had so much fun singing together. We even got matching rings and I still have mine to this day. I miss Sofifi and her laugh every day." Natalia

Sofia wrote this in her *Letter to My Older Self* remembering Ainsley – *"I remember when I randomly started saying "Don't do it!" to Ainsley and she was staring at me and I got nervous and all of a sudden, she reached for my food and I screamed really loud and everyone looked at me. Natalia was in a gymnastics competition and Marie was in the bathroom. They both missed it."*

They loved each other dearly, wrote in each other's *Letters to My Older Self,* and went to four different schools at the end of their middle school career.

All these beautiful friendships drifted away in the background as new characters started to emerge on the scene during high school. The ASC club had faded away and with it all the innocence of that precious time.

Sofia Bella's world changed dramatically when she started high school. She became aware of a new reality away from her catholic faith and the environment of a small school. She never revealed how anxious she was going into high school. She seemed to be doing well and even surprised me by joining the drama club. Now I know she was not as well as she pretended to be. The pressures of this new reality and navigating a new path of self-discovery created confusion and her anxiety worsened.

But, before we move to High School years completely, there are more writings and stories from a younger age to enjoy.

"I don't like adults"

Although she was very funny and playful, Sofia Bella was very selective about who would get her time and affection. She was at times not very expressive, especially with adults outside the immediate family. She would be playing outside and neighbors walking by say, *"Hi Sofia!"*. She would keep her head down and keep doing whatever she was doing with no interest in engaging. She was not rude; she was just not interested.

My mom, Abu Lupe, used to think that Sofia Bella did not like her because she would not talk much with her or want to engage in any games that she would propose. My mom and my sister Rosy used to take her to places like horseback riding or water parks while Sofia visited Puerto Rico. Nothing seemed to be to her liking as long as Abu or Titi Rosy were there. Titi Rosy, though, had two big weapons: twin daughters Monica and Gabriela. When she was with her cousins Moni and Gaby things were different. They were only about 5 years older than Sofia and became her best friends, hence Titi Rosy was able to make her smile for pictures and have a little fun with her as long as Monica and Gabriela were around.

That stubborn little girl was making Grandma feel like she had no hope of ever being in Sofia's good graces. One day, after observing Sofia interacting so well with Carolin, another older cousin, Abu asked; *"Why can you have a conversation with your grown cousin but not with me?"*. She replied, *"I do not like talking with adults."* Abu answered, *"But she is an adult!*". Sofi thought about it and asked, *"How old is Carolin?"* *"Eighteen,"* replied Grandma. Then, the very smart girl who always wanted to win an argument answered, *"Well, I only like talking with kids and adults that are 18 years old."* Abu had no other option but to laugh and keep loving her without pushing her to show her affection back.

Sofia Bella was very clear about her likes and dislikes. When she made up her mind about something or someone there would be no persuasion to make her change her mind and she would always find a justification for it.

Little Sofia (age 4) pretending to kiss aunt Rosy.

Christmas 2020 visiting family in Orlando, Florida.

More Writings Before High School

Acronym for MOTHER

*M*y best mom.

*O*utstanding.

*T*errifying beautiful.

*H*as beautiful dresses.

*E*xcellent.

*R*eads to me every night. (8 years old)

Yesterday, I went to Church in the morning. I saw them light up the candles. I like to see them light the bright candles. I feel holy when they light the beautiful Advent candles. Today is the third week of Advent. One more week!! (to Christmas) (7 years old)

Saint Patrick Church in Wadsworth, IL, and their school were Sofia Bella's second home. She loved everything about her school and church including the fact that the school was small enough that she knew all her classmates. She was happy at Church, especially while ringing the bells as part of the Saint Patrick's Bell Choir. Her Girl Scout meetings and most of her other social activities were at school. When graduating from Middle School and going into High School, she said, *"I know I am going to miss this place. It is so peaceful here."*

Sofia ringing bells for Easter Mass 2018 at St. Patrick's. She was a member of the Bell Choir since she was in third grade. Her last participation was during Christmas 2019 as a freshman in highschool.

Note left at Sofia Bella's funeral by an adult fellow ringer – "*I thought you were great! An inspiration for my own daughter. Thank God that I got to know you in Bell's Choir. I am so sorry to lose you.*" Andrea

I loved guiding her and teaching her ways to put a puzzle together. She got very good at it and it was something that we loved doing together.

One of my main tasks during the evenings besides cooking dinner was assisting with her schoolwork. She will make a summary of chapters at my request and I will quiz her before her tests, especially in Social Studies. She thought history was boring and would argue that we should not care about what happened in the past.

Many times, she came home without the proper books to complete homework. I would contact one of the moms and have her take a picture of the assigned page to send our way. Sofia was grateful that I was able to do that. As the story repeated many times, I grew impatient with her lack of preparation and forgetfulness. She had a school planner where I taught her how to keep track of things. The planner was effective sometimes. I hoped she was going to get better one day, and she eventually did.

Dad was the fun one. When he came home from work, homework was done, gymnastic practices were over, and I was exhausted. During the weekends, Steve and her would go fishing, swimming, and roller skating. They also ran a couple of 5Ks around Thanksgiving time.

In the early years of elementary school, Sofia had this little game with Steve. She pretended to be a girl lost in the woods. She approached Dad and waited until he noticed she was there - sad and lost. They had a whole routine where he was surprised to find such a pretty girl alone in the woods and asked if she was lost. She would nod a yes with her head and they would go on and on until Steve would ask if she was hungry and if she wanted something to eat. It was the sweetest thing.

During this playtime with Dad, her name was Claire. Sometimes Steve brought little Claire to where I was and asked Claire if she wanted to stay with us and be our daughter. She always said yes and we would celebrate this new beautiful girl that was moving in with us. I remember that when Sofia wanted to start the game she would say to Dad, "*Keep doing what you are doing.*" That was code for little Claire to show up. She loved us and trusted us. She was precious in our eyes.

When I read her last poems and read a note left at her funeral by one of her classmates saying "*I heard out her pain, it was torture not being able to change things. … it is easier knowing her pain is over*", it broke my heart. How is it that she preferred to share her pain with others and not with us - with me? Even when she was in therapy, she would not share much with anyone who was prepared to help her navigate her emotions. As a teen, Claire was lost and could not find her way out of the woods to a trusting adult. She stayed-in sharing the misery of being lost with other teens who were lost as well.

If I had superpowers

"*If I had superpowers, my name would be Cylentis. My superpower would be to freeze time. (When someone is in trouble), I could freeze time and somehow get to the person or thing in trouble and take of [sic] it (rescue it). I would say, That's another one saved! I could save the world with these powers.*" (9 years old)

Sofia Bella is now in Heaven, I pray, surrounded by Angels. We ask for her intercession in taking our prayers to Jesus. I've seen things happen where people react to her story by deepening their faith and praying more for themselves or teens/young people they care about. She now has some sort of superpower by having Jesus' ear. How crazy is that?!

Know what's right from wrong

If someone is hurt, call for help or help the person yourself

Never give up on someone

Don't gossip

Never hurts anyone

Even when you are sad, help someone with love

Stand up for someone

Say you are sorry when you do the wrong thing (8 years old)

Self-description pre-middle school — (10 years old)

Super talented

Obsessed with horses

Friend forever

Interesting to talk to

Athletic in all sports

Self-Portrait, 2019-2020

I AM (Sofia Isabella in her own words)

I am funny and creative.

I wonder if I ever going to own a horse.

I hear peace in the world.

I see a horse.

I want to own a horse.

I am funny and creative.

I pretend to ride a horse,

I feel a saddle below me.

I touch a horse's muzzle.

I worry about getting presents done.

I cry when I reflect on my friend's grandpa (Lolo)

I am funny and creative.

I understand I might not own a horse.

I say I want a horse. I dream of having a horse.

I will try to earn a horse,

I hope for a horse.

I am funny and creative.   (9 years old)

Growing Up is Not an Easy Task

One day the horizon was setting. The weather was very rainy. Thunder crackled in the night sky. A bolt of lightning flashed. I was scared. My dad came in the room and comforted me. Then I fell asleep. The next day I was fine and happy. (7 years old)

Sofia was in gymnastics from age 5 to 13 years old. She was very strong and loved hanging upside-down.

We are all afraid of something and look forward to happy things. Sofia Bella was full of life and had many hopes and dreams. The little girl who was looking forward to the magic of Christmas and was afraid of thunder at night could still be found beneath the tough act she put on starting towards the end of Middle School.

Kids in their teen years become fierce and think that they need no more parenting, no more rescuing with a boo-boo buddy or a hug.

Kids in their teen years become fierce and think that they need no more parenting, no more rescuing with a boo-boo buddy or a hug. They are too cool for that. They also think that we are too old to know about their struggles. I said this before but it is worth repeating, trying to be independent is a good thing for our teens. We also need to help them recognize and accept that, for some things, they have to trust us precisely because we are older and have more experience to inform our judgment. This conversation needs to start when they still listen to you and trust in your advice. I started that conversation earlier with my son. The beginning of middle school or even before is a good time.

Life is full of tough choices and options. Life isn't that easy. Sometimes you make mistakes. But that is ok. You can ask God for forgiveness. God always forgives you no matter what you do, where you are, or where are you going. You can always ask God for forgiveness. Nobody is perfect. Let me tell you something AMAZING, God was never born. Isn't that amazing? Jesus is God's son. Jesus died for our sins. If he didn't die, and we were good all our life, we wouldn't go to Heaven, a good place. So, praise God, pray to God, and follow the ten commandments. (7 years old)

Kids see things in simple terms. This is why Jesus said that we must become like children if we want to reach the kingdom of God. He also said, "*Whoever then humbles himself as this child, he is the greatest in the kingdom of Heaven*" (Matthew 18:4)

In the mind of a child, life is so simple: love God and follow the rules. We know that through Jesus' death and resurrection and with God's graces, we will be saved. Yet, as we continue our journey in life, we become doubtful. Teens begin questioning things and tossing what they know to be true in their hearts to the side to follow a more mainstream, culturally accepted, "intellectual" way of thinking. This happened to Sofia Bella. She started to think and dress differently to fit in the more secular world around her when she got to high school. In the process, she stopped believing what she learned early in life about living in harmony with those around you and following the teachings of Jesus while praising God.

Teens begin questioning things and tossing what they know to be true in their hearts to the side to follow a more mainstream, culturally accepted, "intellectual" way of thinking.

All of us, but especially gentle souls like Sofia Bella, were made for more. This world is cruel and living life is at many times painful. Our society has departed so much from what we were created for - to love God, be loved by God, and share this mutual love with those around us.

Unfortunately, as our teens examine the world around them, they try to find answers to their questions in all kinds of places, including their peers. Many times, they do not circle back with adults to gain perspective, as I mentioned earlier. In many circumstances, they end up believing that they were "lied" to and that the world is not as they thought before. This becomes a huge barrier between teens and their parents or caregivers for a while.

This happened to Sofia Bella and to many kids that I have spoken to. One day they start asking questions and people uneducated in matters of faith or with very strict views on how to live our faith throw all kinds of things at these young minds. Suddenly, someone being brought up in faith and loving God becomes agnostic or even atheist. Sofia Bella declared herself agnostic towards the end of freshman year. It is a buzzword these days as many teens and young adults consider themselves as "spiritual but non-religious" or agnostics. They see religion as a belt that tightens them up and they just want to be "free" and do what they feel is "right" for them.

Studies show that if religiosity is experienced as a source of hope and confidence, it reduces the risk of depression in times of mounting stress, facilitates recovery, and diminishes suicide risk.

Why does this matter? Why religion? Studies show that if religiosity is experienced as a source of hope and confidence, it reduces the risk of depression in times of mounting stress, facilitates recovery, and diminishes suicide risk. (Oxford Textbook of Suicidology and Suicide Prevention (1 edn), Chapter 2, *The Role of Religion in Suicide Prevention*)

It is also said that using religion as a source of guilt and fear is not helpful either.

Invite your teen to explore conversations about religion with someone they trust. Having a good understanding of what is and is not about their faith is important. It could be key in coping with uncertainty, anxiety, and other life challenges and can definitely make a difference.

Drawing made at home, first grade, 6 years old.

My Prayer

Dear God, help us all to understand that you are with us all. Help us to turn away from evil. Help the poor from suffering. Help us always to remember that all of us are your children. Help us to learn in school. Help us not to forget you. Help us remember Jesus suffered and died for us. Help us not to say rude words. Thank you for your creation. Thank you (Jesus) for dying for us. Thank you for everything. Amen. (Sofia at 9 years old)

CHAPTER 5

Something Is Not Well

Watching our kids becoming more independent is good and expected. Those changes tell us that our child is developing well but can make us sad at times. Hugs and kisses start to be less frequent. We realize that we are not needed that much, which is also a blessing because an independent person is what we are striving for.

Tweenhood is that awkward period between the ages of around 9 and 12 that marks a significant time for kids going into the next season of life. It is at this tender time, before their teen years, that some kids could start showing signs of possible mental health issues such as depression or anxiety. Add puberty and peer pressure to the mix and you have a better idea of why the teen years are one of the most challenging stages of a person's life. Changes become the norm and are not always well received: changes in responsibilities, their bodies, as well as their perception of authority. Embarrassment makes its entrance at this time and they become self-conscious of everything from the tone of their voice to what they wear to school, and the places they go for fun. It is brutal!

"I make a way for people to access that Kingdom. In this world, bones will still break, hearts will still break, but in the end, the light will overcome darkness."

What is happening with her brain?

During fifth and sixth grades, Sofia Bella was introduced to poetry structure and other technical aspects of this craft. By then she had a large vocabulary. The following poems are from that time. Many of them were created as school projects. Sofia Bella was between 10 and 11 years old at the time she wrote them.

This is a cute little note that melted my heart and was included with a Mother's Day gift for me.

"To a wonderful mother who supports me in school, helps me when I need it, who doesn't hesitate to help those in need and tries her best, and love her family with all her heart."   (10 years old)

Through the years, she grew more fascinated with the idea of Heaven. You will see that in some of her poems, especially the beautifully written *A Glimpse of Heaven*.

Towards the end of 3rd grade in 2014 when she was almost 9 years old, something happened that probably defined the way she related with mental health professionals and mental health in general.

Sofia Bella wrote something about going to Heaven that alarmed her teacher. The teacher was so taken by what Sofia wrote that she quickly sounded the alarm. I was called to meet with the principal that same afternoon.

The prompt for the writing was *"My Dream Vacation."* Sofia wrote that she would love to go to Ireland, France, Florida, and Heaven. She explained in her writing that she would want to go to Florida before Heaven because she did not want to go to Florida as a ghost. To me, it made sense, but the teacher thought that it was too deep and maybe "obscure" for her little mind. For my angel's little mind, it made sense. You go to Heaven when you die, therefore she wanted to visit the other places first, I thought.

When I arrived at the principal's office, I was received by 4 to 5 people. The principal, the social worker, and some teachers. They were all worried and ready to talk with me about the next steps. I felt overwhelmed. What can cause so much commotion regarding the writings of a third grader?

They showed me what she wrote. It was not the body of her work that had everyone concerned but the P.S. and P.P.S. to her work.

P.S. I really do want to kill myself

P.P.S. I'm not useful

In that moment I understood the gravity of the situation and why the teacher assessed that we needed to take some action. The teacher interviewed Sofia before I got to the school. Sofia was asked if she "*had a plan*". Only God knows what all of that meant to my little girl at the time. The truth was that my 9 year/old did not seem to know why she was asked if she "*had a plan*" and why everyone was so alarmed.

Did she mean what she wrote about wanting to kill herself? I was so nervous about the subject that I had difficulties at the time asking plainly what she meant. She was so little and innocent in my mind. I do not remember my conversation with her on the subject. I remember telling her how much she was loved. I also remember going to church right after the meeting and kneeling in front of the Blessed Sacrament. I ended up laying on the floor, face down and full of tears, calling upon God to help me through what was going on. I know God saw me and heard my cries. God was with us through all our ups and downs with our baby girl.

I won't go into much detail but suffice to say that we were asked to take Sofia for a mental health evaluation before she could return to school safely. As you know from a previous chapter, she was not that good about opening up with adults. She resisted the visits with the psychologist as much as she could and barely talked during the sessions. She hated Saturday mornings at that time because we visited the doctor on that day. I tried to make Saturday mornings fun before and after our 45-minute drive to the appointment. All of this as I would take care of Daniel, 5 years younger.

The professional assessment had to be done "quickly" given the situation and the fact that we needed to know if she could return safely back to school. Maybe I was naïve but at the time I did not believe that Sofia wanted to kill herself. Not because I was in denial but because I knew Sofia Bella better than they did. My motherly heart sensed that we were making much of something that, while different from her peers, was normal for her given her sensibility and personality. Regardless, I did what I needed to do to make sure she was fine. Looking back, it was the first visible symptom of a long struggle for her.

At the end of the evaluation process, she was diagnosed with underlying depression that needed no treatment but we needed to *"keep an eye on her."*

It was recommended that Sofia visit the school's social worker weekly and sometimes every other week depending on the resource availability. In February 2017, I received a note from the social worker at school saying that Sofia was not going to be seen by her regularly for the next trimester. Sofia requested to stop the visits as she *"preferred not to have that type of attention drawn to her"*. The social worker made herself available to Sofia for when she needed to process her thoughts. Sofia never went back.

After I learned about her request to stop visits with the social worker, I remember Sofia saying that she felt silly during those meetings. She probably learned to say what was expected to have "good notes" from the social worker. That way it seemed that she was much better and could stop the visits. She did not like to be pulled out of the classroom and be talked about as someone who needs special attention. Yet, she needed that attention. She just didn't want it and decided to deal with things herself. A huge responsibility for a pre-teen. I could not change her mind about it. When I would probe for how were things at school or in general, she would not say much.

In retrospect, that time set a precedent in her mind as she grew older, *"something is wrong with me"*. She wrote once to a friend in high school; *"I heard my mom saying that I was diagnosed with underlying depression. I was not sure of this but I started acting as if it was true."* I was sad to read this.

I later realized that the way she started interacting with mental health professionals possibly set the stage for her lack of engagement with them later when she needed them the most.

We were all trying to do our best to work with her. Our main interest was her wellbeing. I don't share this to say one thing or another. Each situation is different. Only you know what is best for your child because you know them better. Just be open to new and different ideas and research your options. I went right away with the school recommendation without considering Sofia Bella's personality and capabilities or researching different ways to approach the situation. Knowing what I know today, I would do more research before getting her straight to a psychological analysis done quickly due to a *"state of emergency for her safety."* Even if that meant losing days of school.

Given what was going on and the pressures of my very demanding job, I suggested and Steve agreed that I quit my work to pay closer attention to the kids. Spending more time with Sofia and her brother was the best decision at the time. I was overwhelmed. I needed time to regroup and better understand what *"keeping an eye on her"* meant. Reflecting on it, what a blessing that we were able to make such a decision. I recognize that this is not an option for many families. Through that time, I was able to participate in more of their activities, help at school, and treasure many memories that I would have missed. I also have the satisfaction of knowing that I did everything I could to support her in every stage of her life.

Fast Forward to More Mental Health Professionals

During her sessions with the social worker at school, Sofia had shown some difficulty with expressing feelings, and managing emotions as well as her time. She finished Middle School with good grades, was playing soccer in a traveling league, and seemed to be happy.

We decided early on in her school career that Sofia was going to a public school for high school. We wanted her to experience the world outside a Catholic environment in preparation for college and life in general.

Knowing that the change from a small Catholic school to a big public high school could be overwhelming for her, I wanted to do something. The summer before starting high school I suggested taking her to visit a psychologist that worked with teens in the area for a baseline evaluation. Our insurance did not cover mental health visits but I knew it was a necessary step and Steve agreed.

Sofia Bella considered my idea *"a dumb idea, a waste of time and money."* After much back and forth, I convinced her that it would be just one visit to establish her as a "client" in case she needed help in the future. Under that presumption, she went to the appointment. Unfortunately, the appointment lasted only 10-15 minutes. They came out. *"Bella said that she has nothing to share,"* the psychologist said. I used the rest of the time to ask questions about how to better support my teen during this important transition.

I hoped that by establishing a relationship with a mental healthcare professional Sofia Bella would have a safe place to share her fears, anxieties, or anything else coming about from such a big change in her life. She kept saying she was doing well. I sensed that something was brewing but had no idea how fast things were going to get out of hand.

At this time, her "door" was closed but not locked. I could get to her with effort. As time went by it got harder to get to her no matter how patient I was and how much I told her that I loved her no matter what.

Before leaving you with the next group of poems, I want to share with you something that Sofia wrote in fifth grade when she was 10 years old and was learning about Domestic Churches - our homes. She promised the following to her Domestic Church.

For my Domestic Church, I promise to:

- *Mami to try to be good with studying and homework*

- *Daddy to take good care with my glasses*

- *Vale (sister) to try not to fight*

- *Daniel (brother) to be nice*

- *Milo (her doggie) to not hurt you intentionally and to take care of you more*

- *Gigi (first dog) and Nemo (her fish) to see you in Heaven and have a great time*

My Sofia Bella was a gentle soul. Like you and me, she was created to love God and creation and be loved by our Heavenly Father. She had a special connection with things and feelings that other kids her age did not have or were not able to express. She taught us simplicity of life and purity of heart. I miss her tremendously and I can't stop yearning and crying for her every time I look back at the beautiful treasures she left behind with her writings and artwork.

The following poems were written between the ages of 10 and 11 while in fifth and sixth grade. The tenderness and hunger for life were oozing from her pores. Yet, there was something about her that invited unfriendly melancholy to come and visit from time to time even at a tender age.

What If

What if your face was the ocean?

It'd be quite a commotion,

It would be in motion,

What if your face was the ocean?

What if your face was the ocean?

Your eyes could be waves,

With underwater caves,

What if your face was the ocean?

What if your face was the ocean?

People in slow motion,

You must have quite some emotion

What if your face was the ocean?

Limerick

Ella Fitzgerald did sing,

Her voice glided like an eagle's wing,

The crowd went wild,

While she smiled,

And onto her dream she would cling

The Pines

If you were quiet

Enough, still enough, you could

Feel sweet memories

Swirl, winding around the pines

Embedded into your soul

Words

Ode to them, the words

Like fire, burning, burning

In my brain setting

images in a world where

Nothing is impossible

Inspiration Calls

Inspiration calls,

*A voice in my mind,
urging*

Me to change the world

The questions of life

Curious as we wonder

*How, who, when, why,
where*

Sofia in seventh grade playing guitar
after a Girl Scouts meeting. She led
a Merit Badge activity on music.

Breeze

Oh, the breeze whipping

My hair wildly, over

The valley and through

My heart soothing my mind to

Swimming in pools of silence

Rhyming Poem

Everything changes when you come in the room,

It seems that the flowers just started to bloom

In a million years when you weren't here,

You contain love from your hoof to your ear.

Through rain or snow you're always my ride,

Because best friend always stick by their side.

I can't be grateful enough

To have a friend like you, sweet as a creampuff.

Watercolor from around sixth grade (2015-2016). I want to think is her and I.

Ode to horses

Your flowing mane,

Wind winding through your tail

Galloping to freedom

You change my world to love and care,

Leaving warmth everywhere

You nuzzle your muzzle close to my cheek,

Oh, how I love you.

Come closer, my friend, let me love you some more,

Because when I'm feeling down, I hug you tighter than before.

Whether you're angry or calm, sleepy or hyper,

I love you no matter what.

Haikus

Trees like podcast,

Downloading truth to my ears,

They tell me cool stuff.

Nature is precious,

Wild sounds flow through my ears

Animals now roam

The flowers blooming,

Sweet scent of all the pollen

Running through the fields

Repetitive Poem

Galloping Through Life

I gallop gracefully to the garden.

Behind the bushes covered with roses,

red as the apples and Red Sea with Moses.

I gallop gracefully inside the garden.

I gallop gracefully through the garden,

Green leaves and flowers all surround me,

flourishing, blooming, a gorgeous site to see.

I gallop gracefully outside the garden.

CHAPTER 6

Drowning: Transitioning Into High School

Sofia Bella entered High School in the Fall of 2019. No one could imagine what was coming at the end of that year. While there were burning questions in her mind about life in general and a transition into public high school, a virus was cooking somewhere in the world that was going to scar our lives forever. She was full of promise. I think she was excited about the new school, but she was also very nervous.

Her best friends from middle school Marie, Ainsley, and Natalia, tried to stay in touch but life quickly got very busy for each of them as they went about their high school years, each of them in a different school.

> *"Even though I walk through the valley of the shadow of death, I fear no evil; for you are with me; your rod and your staff, they comfort me."*

PSALM 23:4 (NRSV)

The Life She Left Behind

Her middle school graduation was beautiful and was celebrated in the Catholic Church she loved so much, Saint Patrick Church. She was radiant on graduation day. She was happy and was floating around like a butterfly. I took pictures I wanted to take and other pictures she asked me to take with classmates. I was so proud of her. As I look back at that day, I can see light surrounding her. There was something special about her.

That Spring she also did her Confirmation and participated at her school's science fair where she got second place for her poster. Her sister finished Grad School, her brother Daniel did First Communion, and Abu Lupe came from Puerto Rico to be with us through all these events. It was a happy Spring and Summer in our house.

Sofia Bella was sad to leave her St. Pat's family. She loved that she knew everyone and knew what to expect. She once told me that she was not sure how she would feel going to a school that does not require wearing

Sofia with my mom on her Confirmation Day. Spring 2019.

a uniform. Sofia would wear uniform at St. Pat's even on "out-of-uniform" days. She liked traditions and felt comfortable with the routine and familiarity of her school.

As you now know, she was a member of the St. Pat's Bell Choir. She learned how to crochet with her bell choir's teacher, Mrs. Oster. Crochet became one of her hobbies in high school together with drawing, making crafts, and writing. Those things helped her many times when she was under stress or needed a distraction other than her phone. She also learned to play notes on her guitar and taught herself some tunes on her keyboard. Sofia Bella was very talented. She had a beautiful singing and reading voice. She did one of the readings on her Confirmation mass. Her voice was soothing and many were impressed with her talent. I encouraged her to look into a voice-over career. She was intrigued by the prospect.

We provided many outlets for her to be creative and express herself.

When Sofia Bella became a cheerleader for the St. Pat's Basketball team in 8th grade, she did not care that the other girls had their routines down and their own "thing" going on. She wanted to be on the team, and she was. I loved watching her cheering. She loved the uniform. She was a very passionate cheerleader, strong but graceful. I had a front seat to all of her participation and helped prepare her hair before the games.

Sofia pushed us to get her into soccer towards the end of sixth grade. *"My friends are going,"* she said. She joined the Lindenhurst Area Soccer Club (LASC) traveling league. She enjoyed the game and was very responsible with practice. She thrived and

Last Boy's Basketball game St. Pats 2019.

gained skill and agility as time went by. She later tried out for soccer in High School and made the freshman team.

Before going into High School, she was content and seemed happy with her three best friends from St. Pats; Natalia, Ainsley, and Marie. The four of them enjoyed a day in the city of Chicago, including a Lake Michigan boat trip, as part of their graduation activities. During the Spring, I organized for the four of them to go with their moms to see the Broadway play Hamilton. Sofia had memorized most of Hamilton's lyrics. She beamed joyfully that day and was singing along. That girl could rap and sing most of the songs from the musical with a speed and grace that would impress even those who did not like musicals or rap that much.

She still was very close to her two best friends from the neighborhood: Czarlize and Arriana. Arriana was looking forward to having Sofia Bella in the same school for the first time.

At this time, I was working a part-time job that was less demanding with fewer hours than my previous jobs. Life felt good to me at the time. Although reading through her things after she was gone, I learned that she was anxious about the new school and extremely sad to leave Saint Pat's. I wish she made her fears known at the time but she was not much of a talker, not with me. I just want to hug that eighth-grader one more time right now.

I spoke earlier about the devastation that COVID-19 brought to all of us, especially to our kids. Sofia Bella, and those of her generation, dealt with unimaginable challenges. She was sensitive to all of it and carried all her worries and growing anxieties within.

By the end of her first semester in high school and before schools closed due to COVID-19, she was getting comfortable with her new school, enjoying a theater class, practicing soccer, and making auditions for the Speech and Drama Clubs. She was embracing her new life and making new friends.

It was at this time also that Sofia started to express questions about her identity, her sexuality, and God. She engaged in political debates in school and on social media regarding the 2020 Presidential election. She joined forums with her friends in Discord, a website to "hang out" while playing games, and engaged in all kinds of conversations while playing *Minecraft* and *The Legend of Zelda*.

During the short time that Sofia Bella was in high school, she gained many new friends. Her circle was small but tight. They loved doing things together. There was a lot of drama between them from time to time, as always happens at this age.

COVID-19 took all of that away from her. Classrooms were now opened through a computer screen and many kids, including herself, hid behind a dark screen not even wanting to turn on their cameras. Soon, she started to sleep through the classes and I started getting emails to make sure that Sofia was in class, camera on, and participating. It was a struggle for her to participate and for me to keep her motivated. As months went by, she was less able to keep up with schoolwork.

School during COVID - Spring of 2020, Freshman year.

And finally, it's all too much. I crawl into my bed as the tears start falling and my face contorts into an ugly expression. I curl up on my side into a ball and a silent scream escapes my lips. I am in agony, but I must suffer in silence and in darkness because if I make a sound, they will surely find me. So, I sob in silence as the pain grows in my chest. My arms wrap around my torso. I've been crying every night in my bed for about a month now, but the pain never subsides. I don't feel anything now; I lay motionless.

Written by Sofia sometime towards the end of middle school.

The Silent Treatment

My first daughter was 12 years old when Sofia was born. I was happy to have another girl to share stories with, go shopping, watch movies, go to the theater, cook with me, help with cleaning the house, and much more once.

In middle school, Sofia spent most of her time reading and writing stories. She asked Steve many times to read some of them and would often ask if we thought she could publish her stories and if they could be in the library for others to read. She loved visiting the library! We always encouraged her and instilled confidence in her many talents. At some point, she became a contributor writer to our neighborhood newsletter writing articles on different topics. Following my recommendation, she brought the articles to school earning her a certificate as a published author from her librarian. She was so proud of her accomplishment and took her responsibilities as a reporter very seriously.

In high school, she still loved visiting the library but would not share with us any of her writings. She would hide her writing and drawings from us. She never showed us her Speech Club speeches or wanted us to go to her competitions. She convinced me that parents were not allowed. I learned later that it was not true.

Sofia came home to a home-cooked meal. She arrived home about half an hour before Daniel. *"How was your day, Sof?"*, I would ask. *"Good,"* she would reply. She served her portion and ate quietly, listening to her music, or scrolling through her phone. I wanted to know more about her day but she did not say anything else or she would give me a short answer to any other question. She was never unpolite or vicious towards me but liked to keep her distance.

After she was done with her meal, she would go to her room until Steve was back home from work. He would call her out of her room to come down to the family room area. She would ask, *"Whyyyy?"* He would respond, *"Because I want to see my daughter. Come and say hi! I have not seen you in all day"*. He would also ask about her day with less success in getting responses and she quickly would go back to her room. Eventually, she would come down to the kitchen for a snack when we were already in our room getting ready for bed. By this time in her life, we were *"them"* and she did not like spending time with *"them"* or her brother.

Here is a note/poem that Sofia wrote for her brother reminding him to stay away from her room. She was almost a seventh grader when she wrote this.

Privacy

*I know you went in my room
again*

I know you took my pen.

*I don't know why or how or
when,*

*But with innocence you
can't blend.*

*Maybe we should lock the
door so you*

In this picture, Daniel is 4 years old and Sofia is 9 years old.

Can't come to my room anymore,

Taking stuff from off my floor,

You won't come in my room - I am sure.

While in her room, she would work on some art projects, draw in her notebooks while listening to music, crochet, play her guitar, sometimes sing out loud, or we could hear her having conversations with friends and laughing hysterically. In her room, she was a different person than when she was with us. More friendly and easygoing with her friends. Silent treatment for us and anyone who could make a difference in her treatment.

The Storm in Full Swing

The following writings are from later on, between freshman and junior years. Ages 14 to 16 years old, 2019 through 2021.

I found most of these writings after she passed. The first couple of weeks after everything settled, I went through her computer files, phone, social media, and anything that I could get my hands on that could give me a clue of why things went the way they did. It was a painful and long process but it helped me to gain a better understanding of her state of mind. It became a sacred place and time for me to grieve that was only hers and mine.

I wanted to try to understand why she was gone. after all of us, including herself, thought that the medicines were working and things were getting better.

Always trying to work with her, I made an effort to meet her friends and invite them home. They were her rock at the time, more than I was. It was precisely because I knew and had good relationships with some of her high school friends that I was able to get access to writings that she had deleted from her computer or phone. Many of the pieces I will share next came from Kelsey. This friend was mature beyond her years and provided good insights and support for Sofia Bella, especially during her first year in high school.

Some of her work has no title or date. If there was no title, I marked it *"Untitled"*. I will never match her creativity therefore I will not attempt to title her work. If I have a date, I provide it. Otherwise, know that I found it or it was given to me without a date. I will also, when needed, provide a bit of context.

Detective Nose
Written on October 31st, 2019. Collected from Kelsey

I smell brownies. Mother?

Perhaps she has decided to bake yet another batch.

Allow me to investigate.

Spy mission: commence.

As I move closer to the scent, it changes. It is now a rich garlicky smell rather than a moist, chocolatey smell.

I suspect garlic bread.

I initially suspected my mother was baking brownies. Currently I suspect garlic bread. Is that clear?

I believe I heard the beep of the oven. Perhaps I stand by my initial suspicions?

("maybe ask her") One must never reveal themself whilst on a mission. This is common knowledge.

I shall now step out of my room and further investigate.

The smell is intensifying.

The smell of garlicky brownies fills my nose. It is quite peculiar.

I have successfully exited the room.

I see a cooking pan.

I have successfully defended [sic] the stairs without notice.

The investigation was successful.

The oven was being rid of heat but the pan contained no food except oil.

No other freshly baked goods were visible.

Alas I have forgotten to check the oven toaster. Perhaps garlic bread awaits there.

Sofia Bella suffered from insomnia. This is a typical symptom that accompanies depression and anxiety disorders. It is exacerbated by being on the screen for many hours, especially right before going to bed. Sofia and I talked many times about developing a healthier routine to go to bed. It is hard for teens to get off their phones, but it is so important for their brain and overall development and mental health.

Unfortunately, it became a vicious cycle. She could not go to sleep, so she would turn to her phone or school Chromebook. This kept her awake even longer. Sometimes I would go to her room later at night and find her finally asleep with the screen of her computer open facing her. I would close the computer and kiss my baby goodnight.

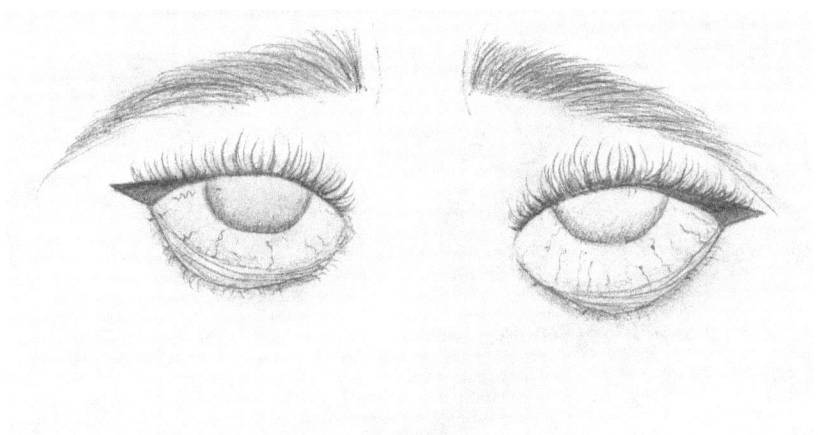

November 4th, 2019 at 11:06 pm

Bella: *"I am unable to slip into the mansions of rest, stuck between consciousness and unconsciousness. Every second my body feels obligated to move, as if an invisible force is moving it around for the sole purpose of keeping me awake. My throat is dry and longs for the sweet relief of water, and sweat collects on my forehead. I am being tortured by insomnia. My eyelids are heavy but refuse to stay shut. My mind is tired but refuses to stay silent. It screams out cries of desperation and frustration. Poetry may be my only temporary escape from the hands of torture that claw at my eyes and my mouth, forcing my mind to remain awake."*

Untitled

The great moon. Soon it will hear the tune of people dying.

The moon listens as they glisten with blood.

A flood from an open wound. It'll all be over soon.

The mud and the earth, the sand and the dirt all listen and watch

And wait.

Anticipation for the population and its creations to disappear.

But they'll still be here. Year after year, they'll continue to smear the earth's great surface.

The sun will wait for the chaos to become undone.

Nobody won. We lay in a mess of

human.

It's over.

The moon, the mud and the earth, the sand and the dirt,

And the sun watched us grow. They would have watched us tomorrow.

If we were still alive.

Sofia Bella was introspective and introverted. She would not be the type of girl who looked for conversation in a group of strangers. She would prefer sitting by herself even if no one approached her at all. Yet, she had this magnetism that attracted people to her. Once a peer approaches her and strikes up a conversation, she engages and they are strangers no more. This is how she made one of her first friends in high school, Kelsey, as a freshman in her theater class.

When Sofia Bella said that she was going to take drama, I was both surprised and happy. I was a drama club member and theater lover myself back in high school. I could not believe that my Sofia was intrigued by the idea of being part of the theater crowd. I said to myself, "*Great! I'll take it. This is going to help her to open up more and make some friends*".

Her first audition came right away and she was picked to be part of the ensemble. She did not want me to watch her rehearsals. The day of the show finally came for *The Lion King* musical. When she entered dancing with the rest of the ensemble, smiling, and moving with confidence, I could not believe my eyes. "*That's my Sofi!*" I was so proud. My little flower bud was opening up into an amazing fragranced flower and I was there to witness it. She was amazing dancing side by side with her new friend Kelsey. I will forever be grateful to this caring teen who extended herself to Sofia when she was a loner in her drama class.

Kelsey left this note for her at the funeral – "*Bella loved art. We were in theater class together and I remember she sat alone the first day. I sat next to her the second day and we clicked. She would send me videos of her singing, the poems she wrote, and some art she made. I will never forget her endless creativity and imagination. I love you, Bella.*"

Kelsey also sent the following conversation with a note for me – The note said: "*This is a very insightful conversation we had as she wondered existential questions.*"

December 1st, 2019 at 11:58 pm (Sent to me by Kelsey)

Bella: *Kelsey, have you ever thought about "instant deaths"? when someone is driving their car and they get into a car accident, sometimes their death is so quick that it's called an instant death. but what about that one split second when your lungs are imploding and your rib cage and collarbone are being crushed and cracked into many small pieces inside your body? what about that utter, raging, pure agony controlling your every move? the pain that was once unfathomable to your mind now reveals itself through a raging fire that is coursing through every fiber of your body. your actions become mere reactions to that seemingly impossible pain. just in that small instant. people say that they would like to die by instant death. they do not know the price they would pay. even if that price lasted one second.*

December 1st, 2019 at 12:25 am

Bella: *you know one day we're gonna like die and people will forget our very existence and in approximately one hundred years, the thought of our being will never once cross anyone's mind and if we don't do something incredibly impactful to the world, then what's the point of being nice or going the extra mile or joining the soccer team? what's the point of doing that one kind gesture to that old man? he will die, too, probably faster than you will, and it won't matter, in the end. almost nothing will.*

Kelsey: the point is for you and other people. for the now. sure people may not remember your name in 100 years, but what if they do? and if they don't, so what? you still existed. you will still exist in the earth and

Self-portrait in pencil drawn around 2020. She loved
her hair made up in two French braids.

all around. everything you do matters, if not for the people later, then for the people now. the people we are reading about in history probably never thought they'd be talked about thousands of years after their deaths. mere poets and philosophers. yet they are and will be. celebrities will be talked about, and everyone get their 15 minutes of fame sometime in their life where someone sees them, and knows of them and cares. so everything does matter. especially you.

Bella: *yeah but they were super cool and smart and they DID do something incredibly impactful to the world. but if you're not smart or athletic or special to society then there's no point for you to try to do anything special at all because it won't end up changing anything.*

but perhaps my points and thoughts are entirely focused on the importance of impacting society. perhaps one may see through eyes that hold other priorities. perhaps, if i saw the world through different eyes, i wouldn't be saying these things. but, since my mind is the way it is, naturally prioritizing one thing over another, i am arguing for my side. my eyes long for rest but my mind lies wide awake. this is an interesting combination, and it brings out my poetic and deep-thinking side of myself. i have also been reading some John Green lately, so perhaps that has contributed to my behavior. nevertheless, apologies to you, friend, for interrupting whatever you may have been doing prior to this conversation.

Kelsey: but you're forgetting that anyone can impact society and do something important, even without realizing it. thousands of people are doing it right now through social media. even if the queen of England doesn't know your name, maybe 1000 do. think of everybody that you've ever met. you have probably impacted their life in some way or another, even as a cashier or pedestrian. it may not always seen like it, but people listen. people watch and they remember. even if you aren't in the textbooks, you could be in peoples' minds, in their stories. if you would like to see the world through a different perspective, we could have a really good talk if you came over sometime probably over winter break.

December 23rd, 2019 at 11:37 pm – (From Sofia to Kelsey)

Bella: *concerning one of my previous thoughts: i continue to stand by my original words regarding the question "if you're not going to make a significant impact on anything that lasts (such as the world), what's the point in trying hard in anything at all?". what is the point of doing anything if you know you're not going to be important or revolutionize anything? Thomas Edison:*

inventor, scientist, and many more. he changed the way people think forever. he made an important change in the world. whereas i, who most likely won't do anything as such, will probably be forgotten in a century or two. the world will move on and i will no longer cross the mind of any human being. i will be a blade of grass in the Plain of Forgotten Ideas, like many, many others. assuming i don't do anything amazing, whatever is the difference between me dying naturally in around eighty years or me dying right now? there is no difference. what is the point of living anymore? i read a beautifully written poem and one of the lines read, "we can only build sandcastles where the sand is wet. but where the sand is wet, the tide comes." this perfectly portrays my idea. there is no reason to build sandcastles in the first place if the tide will eventually destroy it. again, perhaps i would think differently if my mind was someone else's. my thoughts are based on "whatever is temporary is (ultimately) unimportant". but maybe if my mind thought in a different way, my views would not be the same.

thanks for reading,

Wexler

 Insight: There were 2 Sofias and 3 Bellas in her small group of friends. Her friends started calling her by her last name, Wexler, to differentiate her from the other Bellas' in their small group of friends.

Self-harm is No Joke

i've been keeping this secret from my parents from [sic] years and they found the goddamn razor blade and i lied but then i burst into tears and i can't believe they found out and they said they're gonna get me help but i don't want to go to a psychologist i just want them to leave me alone

Later I found Kelsey's responses to this message from Sofia Bella. Kelsey encouraged her to welcome therapy and to speak openly with a professional about this unhealthy habit. She also told Sofia that we (her parents) were alarmed for a good reason and that we were trying to help her.

As parents, we must prepare with knowledge of mental health, including the habit of cutting or self-harm.

As parents, we must prepare with knowledge of mental health, including the habit of cutting or self-harm. In the same way, we prepare for how to feed the baby and deal with a fever or ear infection, we need to prepare for the possibility of some level of mental illness in our teens. We should be able to identify signs and symptoms of different unhealthy behaviors. It is that important.

Self-harm is a manifestation of something bigger happening and most of the time is related to their state of mental health. Some reasons why teens may choose to "cut" or self-harm include difficulty understanding or expressing emotions, not knowing how to cope with personal trauma, feelings of rejection, self-hatred, anger, and similar emotional states.

Teens are "cutting" as a way to shift the focus from their pain inside towards something else. When you read about "cutting", you learn that when someone engages in self-harming the hormone endorphin is released. This hormone is naturally produced and it is released within the brain and nervous system when a person feels pain or stress. Endorphins relieve pain, reduce stress, and provide a sense of well-being. Endorphins are similar in chemical structure to an opioid pain reliever. They are also known as "feel-good" chemicals because they make you feel better in the moment. Unfortunately, with time, teens need more and more of the "cutting" to feel the same effect, trapping them in a vicious cycle. For more information, I recommend a book I read - *Hope and Healing for Kids Who Cut* by Marv Penner.

Teens are "cutting" as a way to shift the focus from their pain inside towards something else.

There are ways to produce the same effect by healthier means. Exercising is one of them. Exercising will give you the same "feel-good" sense by releasing endorphins but it requires having the energy to exercise to the point of releasing them. This is hard to do for teens suffering from depression or anxiety disorder. Many schools are emphasizing the importance of getting involved in physical and other extracurricular activities to push teens to find ways to release such endorphins supporting mental health through healthier habits. Find out what programs are available in your teen's school and nudge them into one activity that is fun for them.

Exercising will give you the same "feel-good" sense by releasing endorphins.

Insecurity and Anxiety, Who Came First the Egg or the Chicken

A teen with mental illness will show many different signs that something is not well. Self-harming is only one way. Self-doubt, negative self-talk, lack of concentration, and anxiety are only a handful of symptoms that can show up. Sofia Bella battled these symptoms and a few more. Was she anxious because she thought so little of herself or was her self-expectation so high that made her anxious? It is hard to know. Mental illness needs to be addressed with a mental health professional. Please do not wait. You do not have insurance? Find resources available in the community. Read the last chapter on resources.

Untitled

(found in a notebook, she also sent this to a couple of her friends. There was a friend in her small group that she liked but he was only interested in her as a friend. I think she wrote this to him.)

I am a sunflower

Kinda'

Funny

If I were a

Rose,

Maybe you'd

PICK

Me

I don't know when Sofia Bella started to feel so insecure and tiny that she just wanted to fade away. It seems that everything started as a small snowball when she was in grade school that grew slowly first and faster towards her teen years. It got so big that it finally burst in the worst way possible due to her inability to engage with therapy.

I remember driving her to meet with friends at a nearby forest preserve, Independence Grove, in the Spring of 2021. We were all masked up even though we were meeting in an open space. She could only stay for a few hours due to another commitment we had. Rather than saying no to her asking to join her friends, I decided to drive her and bring a book to read while waiting for her. I knew spending time with her friends was not only important to her but a good thing for her mental health.

As I drove her, I noticed she was anxious. Her crossed leg moving constantly up and down in a race to nowhere. I asked, "*Why are you nervous?*" She replied, "*I am not nervous.*" "*Why are you swinging your leg so fast? Can you stay still?*" Sofia answered, "*I can't stop it. I know we are not late but I feel as if we are going to arrive late, I can't help it. It always happens to me. I am always afraid of being late for things even when I know I am not late.*"

Sofia was letting me into her world if only for a few seconds!

I reassured her that we were well on time. We were the first ones to arrive. When everyone arrived, they rented pedal boats and had fun enjoying the fresh air and laughing together. When it was our time to leave, I texted her. Her pedal boat approached the area where I was and she jumped out. She was content and relaxed during our drive back home. She did not say much about the time with her friends. I asked, "*Did you have fun?*" "*Yeah*", she replied but did not share anything else. I was happy knowing she spent time doing something she loved which was having fun with her close friends. When we got home and as she was leaving the car she said; "*thank you ma'.*" I said, "*Thank you for what?*". She replied, "*Thank you for driving me.*" "*Sure sweetie*", I replied. It was a good morning for both of us.

As you know, Sofia Bella loved poems, songs, and reading good books. Reading and theater were two ways she had to find a happy place when she could find the energy. I imagine that this poem by Christy Ann Martine caught her attention. I found it on her computer. I want to think that somehow I was meant to find it. It soothes my soul.

She's in the Sun, the Wind, the Rain

She is in the sun,
the wind, the rain.
She's in the air you breathe with
every breath you take.
She sings a song of hope and cheer,
there's no more pain, no more fear.
You'll see her in the clouds above,
hear her whisper words of love,
you'll be together before long,
until then listen for her song.

By Christy Ann Martine

A Radical Change

Her unwillingness to engage in conversations with adults made the work of her therapists and doctors especially challenging. The school social workers during freshman and sophomore years, for the most part, would reply to my pleading to check on her more often with something like *"She knows she can come to me if she needs help or if she is feeling anxious. She knows my door is open."* I would argue with them over the phone about their approach. I knew Sofia was not going to knock on their doors. A lot of my time and energy went into fighting the status quo of the pandemic and finding ways to help her and advocate for her.

Why are they not doing something else? I thought it was such a passive approach to manage students who were hurting so much, especially through and after COVID and the stupid lockdowns. Her school was also a big public school with limited mental health resources to deal with a massive number of students drowning in their silence. It was not business as usual and, in my opinion, they were not grasping the severity and intensity of it all.

Looking back, I feel that I made a lot of noise and exhausted myself without affecting much change. I felt like the Israelites against Goliath, afraid and not knowing what else to do. I felt alone in my fight with most places shut down due to COVID restrictions and Steve working long hours.

She was not having meals at the same time we did and would refer to her family as "*them*" when talking with others about us. She would refer to her dad during this time as her "*biological father*," as if she had any other father on earth. She was so convincing in stating the "*biological father*" status for her dad that at some point the hospital's social worker asked where was her biological dad and who was then living in the house.

By the second semester of sophomore year, she was barely talking with any of us in the immediate family. The weeks leading to the Christmas in 2020 were a nightmare. Police were involved and Sofia had to spend a few days right before Christmas with the neighbors. I was at a breaking point; Steve did not know how to handle Sofia and would make things worse. Daniel was caught in the middle of it all.

Sofia's relationship with her dad deteriorated a lot at this time. After some outbursts towards Sofia for her lack of help around the house or her constant isolation from her family, Steve would come back to her asking for forgiveness for losing his temper. She saw we were human, made mistakes, and asked for forgiveness. We were all learning to live in our new reality managing mental health issues. All of us needed help in one way or another.

Even through hard times, Steve would take her out for ice cream, her favorite treat, when picking her up from a friend's house or a rehearsal at school. Sometimes you can hear them playing guitar together or Sofia showing off a new segment of music she self-taught on the keyboard. At times he asked her to help change the car's engine oil to get her out of her room and she would accept. Sofia needed time to come around and we just had to keep patiently loving her and waiting while therapy and medicines finally would make things better for her.

At this time, we were not pushing her to go to church as we were at the beginning. We always reminded her of God's love and how much we loved her regardless of what we were going through. We did this through notes, cards, words, and acts of kindness toward her. On my personal Facebook page, you can find the last birthday card I gave her. She was turning 16 years old. It is pinned at the beginning of my page so I can find it easily. When I found the card in her room after she was gone, I realized that the picture on the card was telling of what was to come in a very aery way.

Sofia and I had conversations about her feelings regarding liking people of her same sex at the same time she liked boys. She knew she did not have to go to college if she did not want to. We explored scenarios of her going to a Junior College, taking a year off, or becoming a dog groomer as she was so good with training and attending to Milo. We explored possible college careers. She was looking into psychology or sociology the last time we spoke about it and drew pros and cons on my whiteboard. She knew I loved her and supported her no matter what. She was my baby. How could I not love her and protect her? We would have good, productive, thought-provoking conversations only to have her retrieve quickly back to her inner cave.

Unfortunately, she was not getting the help she needed due to her lack of desire to work with her therapist. We were all trying to better understand the situation and reach out to her in more effective ways not knowing that we were running out of time.

My Friend Says, "No More Religion for Me"

At this time, she openly declared herself agnostic. How does a God-loving, sensitive, spiritual person go to such a declaration? Some of it is because of the culture, the movies we watch, the songs we listen to, the books we read, and the ones that we stop read-ing. Sometimes people stay agnostic until later or even for their entire lives. For others, it is just a season  where they are trying to figure out things and find God on their terms and in a way that speaks to them. With love, patience, and prayers, I was hoping that the latter was her case and that the season would be over at some point in her life. I prayed over her many times while she was sleeping.

She met an atheist classmate during her freshman year who became her friend and was very convincing with his arguments. With him, Sofia went from doubting God to believing that religion was a "fantasy" and that all the talk about Jesus was, as he would say, "pure mumbo-jumbo." She also started to think that there was no life after death and, therefore no Heaven. This thought drove her closer to thoughts of dying. "If there is nothing after, why wait?", she said in a self-recorded video I found.

I remember once coming to Sofia Bella's room and finding her in her walk-in closet connected to Discord, a chatting platform for gamers, having a conversation with friends. I was checking on her as I always did for her safety. I said "*hi*" to anyone online. Unaware of who was on the line, I simply asked who was on the call. Few said their names and said hi back to me. I assumed some others stayed quiet in the background.

Sofia's atheist friend took the lead in the conversation. I've talked with him before. He has visited our house and even helped Sofia to clean her room once along with other friends. He had a great deal of influence on Sofia, I thought. I always tried my best to invite him to the house and get to know him better. One time I even asked him to help me with Sofia's organization with school-related tasks and to inspire her to take better care of her schoolwork. He was very smart, had academic excellence, worked hard, was organized, and was very outspoken. He probably is to this day. He was also funny and it seemed that Sofia liked to be around him.

In this particular online conversation, the courteous greetings very quickly turned into him versus her conversation. His point of view versus mine regarding religion. He took the command and started telling me how I was not doing good by "Wexler," as he called Sofia Bella. He said that I needed to "*let Wexler be and stop shoving religion down her throat.*" I remember thinking, where is this coming from? I was taken aback by what this kid was saying. I figured that Sofia Bella probably had conversations with him about her not wanting to go to mass anymore and how we were not accepting her decision. Sofia was by my side, silent. I was surrounded by her clothes, her staring at the computer without saying a word, and many ears on the line listening. No one else said a word in favor or against it. It became a debate of two viewpoints, mine and that of a 15-year-old high schooler.

I kept my cool. I felt it was a teachable moment for my Sofia Bella on how to manage differences with love and also strength and conviction. I also realized that this kid was allowing me to somehow speak to her about the "*why*" of our position since she never wanted to hear about it. I wanted to clearly say to her, and all of those listening, why we were not letting her forget the faith that served her so well for almost her entire life.

I am so grateful for the Holy Spirit guiding me in that moment. My faith was strong and my love for Sofia Bella and desire to protect her was stronger. With compassion, I responded with something like this:

"I love Sofia. She is my child. God entrusted her to me to love her, educate her, and guide her in her journey through life. I believe that there is life after death. Heaven is real. I feel responsible for the eternal life of Sofia's soul the same way I am responsible for her physical and mental health on this earth. For that reason, I can't just let her walk away from her faith while she is a child under my care. Think about this, if Sofia says one day to me, "Mom I want to jump off a bridge to see what happens", do you think I would let her jump knowing that she could hurt badly, or worse die, just because she wants to and she feels it is right for her? You bet I won't. Neither would any other parent I know. Letting her walk away from her faith, to us, is like letting her walk towards a sure death – the death of her soul. I would not do that to her. Once she is an adult, she can do what she wants, and it will be on her but not while under my loving care. Can you see this?"

There was silence. Sofia said absolutely nothing in favor or against what I said or what her friend argued. I said goodnight to everyone and told them that they were all good kids. In my mind and to avoid more conflict, I said *"I will pray for all of you as I keep praying for my Sofia Bella"* and left the room.

Sofia and I never talked about this at a later time. She never told me how she felt. I was hoping that it was one of those things we would talk about when she was a grown woman and I was much older. I know the Holy Spirit guided my answer and the tone of my voice. I wanted to be a loving adult for them without abandoning my convictions. I would never know what impact the conversation had on those quietly listening. I pray for all of the youth often and they are included in my prayers.

My Sister Is Not My Sister

One day we were having a *"family intervention"* over the phone during her last hospital stay in October 2021. The counselor asked Sofia Bella, do you have relationship problems with anyone in your family? Sofia Bella answered, *"Yes."* The counselor pressed further, *"With whom?"* She replied, *"With all of them."* I intervened, *"Are you sure Sofia? What about your sister?"* She thought about it and came back quickly with a, *"She is not family!"* I said, *"But she is your sister"*. She thought again, *"Well, she is different."* Her sister was not living at home at the time and was her half-sister. They were communicating more at that time and trusted each other more than they trusted me. I was good with that. They had each other and I was meant to stay in the background as it happens when our children grow old. In Sofia's mind, her sister was a helpful friend, not an adult. She was not part of her very *"problematic family."* Her sister was not *"them"*.

It is curious how perceptions and realities of one's life are so distorted when you suffer some kind of mental illness. Did she have reasons to be mad at us parents? Yes! I was mad at my dad when I was her age and so was her dad. But in her mind, it was more than feeling mad, we were the enemy and she wanted to avoid us at all costs.

My Mom Is a Raccoon

Ready for a funny story? I remember that in the same phone conversation with the social worker, she called me a raccoon. I happen to think that raccoons are cute, so I was not offended.

During the last six months or so before her hospital stays began, Sofia Bella was throwing a lot of her things in the garbage. Encouraging posters were coming off the walls and so were pictures from her middle school and neighborhood friends. Some of her recognition certificates together with drawings and writings were landing in her garbage can or burnt. She would toss it all without any regard. I later read in some books that this could be a sign of someone who is contemplating suicide, has resolved to go through with it, and is clearing out their space by throwing or giving away their possessions.

Not knowing the reason why, she was getting rid of such things, I rescued some and placed them in a memory box for her to have later in life. I had conversations with her about how she should save some of her work to enjoy later and remember her thoughts and feelings at the time. I made it a habit to go over her garbage every so often, especially if it was overflowing, to rescue some things I thought she could appreciate having in the future. This is why she accused me during the family call of going over her garbage like a raccoon. Hence, the title of raccoon that I wore proudly that day with no shame.

Sofia Bella's Aching Soul Poured into Poetry

The following set of poems reflects a crescendo of a desire to die but still holding on and pleading with "someone" who was "*the only person*" who could save her. I do not know for sure who she was referring to. These were written around six to nine months before she passed, maybe less.

I read them for the first time about a week or two after her funeral. I felt so much compassion for her hurting soul. Melancholy had taken residency in her mind and she refused to engage fully in psychotherapy.

guitarist

my hands were poised, the stage was set

the strings were still, capo on fret

my fingers danced on the guitar

the strings cried out a loud hurrah

my hands moved on their own, it seemed

the wood produced a charming gleam

each vibration produced a sound

that filled the air–– free, unbound

and lastly, with my final strum

my melody became undone.

my sea

i struck my knife upon my heart

and then the storm had ceased

the waves retired, no longer high

a mist of soothing peace

the vivid lightning was no more

its light no longer flashed

the thunder stopped its booming cry

the sea a tinted
glass

my death somehow
awakened me

although i am
asleep

a new life in my
nothingness

there's nothing
more i seek

trade

she offered you a trade

two hours for a million years

you ignored her every word

so, she took her million years and gave them to the devil

now she's underground

still thinking about you

how you didn't care for her million years

i think you should have listened

but who am i?

two hours

if you stayed up for two more hours

and sacrificed a bit of sleep

she'd still be right here in your arms

don't come to me to sob and weep

it would've taken just your time

to make sure she was doing fine

two hours to keep her alive

but you ignored her every sign

you disregarded cries for help

when she would reach her hand to you

when she would tell you she was scared

of the things she thought she would do

all she wanted was someone

to stop her from her deadly crimes

all she needed was someone

to help her get the rope untied

two hours of your precious time

was that too much to ask of you?

two hours for a million years

I suppose you'll see her soon

River

what a beautiful river that flows down my arm

back in the psych ward, they call it self-harm

branches flow into one stream of red

gushing as i think of the words he said

the river grows

my arm is red

if this keeps up,

soon, i'll be dead

but i don't mind

it's not like he

really would have

wanted me

to stay with him

he doesn't care

and while i bleed

it seems to stare

the cut i made

half an inch deep

i feel nothing

i cannot weep

as my own blood makes its way to the ground

so does my body; i've finally found

the place i belong— it's not on this earth

in the darkness begins my new birth

You Could Have Saved Her

She died thinking nobody loved her

She died thinking she was alone

She died thinking there was no one there to save her

But you could have saved her

You could have pulled her up from the raging ocean and offer her a life vest

But you didn't

You ignored

And you waved away

Any cry for help

And she fucking drowned

And

You

Could

Have

Saved

Her

Last Dance in the Darkness

One night in October 2021, after two hospital stays, Steve and I were getting ready for bed. It was almost one in the morning. The sensor for the front porch camera went off. Steve looked at his phone. *"Jessie is here!"*, he said surprised. Why would Sofia's school friend be at our door at this time? He started ringing the doorbell franticly. We came running to the door. As soon as we opened, Jessie desperately pleaded, *"We need to stop her - she is going to do it!"* *"Do what"*, I nervously asked. He was so agitated that he could barely talk further. I ran up to her room. There she was, still, seated on her bed, lights on, and with no facial expression. I was puzzled.

I said, *"Sofi, Jessie is here for you. Do you know why?"* She did not reply and kept staring forward. I said, *"Go and see what he wants."* Sofia went down to meet with Jessie. I left them in the kitchen as Steve and I gave them some space unaware of what was going on. The doorbell was ringing again. It was Jessie's mom. She seemed also very disturbed and anxious. She calmed herself down and started telling us what was going on. *"Bella is trying to kill herself."*, she explained, *"and Jessie got in the car and left quickly to stop her*". His mom said that he left so quickly that she could not join him. She changed her clothes and drove to our house as soon as she could.

I called Sofia from the kitchen. We sat on the stairs leading to the second floor. I asked, "*Sofia, mamita, is it true that you told Jessie that you wanted to end your life tonight?*" She would not say anything. I insisted, "*Are you not feeling safe? Should I call 911?*" She kept silent.

 Insight: I did not know at the time about the Suicide crisis-specific line 988. That is the line that needs to be called in these cases. It is a newer dedicated line.

In the meantime, Jessie's mom went with Steve to the kitchen while I was talking with Sofia. I felt scared and powerless. I wanted to get through to her but she did not want to share what was going on in her mind. She would not say why she was feeling the way she was feeling or why she said she wanted to stop living. I did not want to upset her. I wanted so hard to work with her. I remember keeping my cool and calmly saying again, "*Maybe it is better if you go to the Emergency room and they check on you.*" With a very low voice, she started pleading with me not to call 911. "*I am ok ma'. I don't want to miss more school*", she said. I wanted to believe that she was doing better but that was not the case. Her plea changed into begging me not to call the emergency line. I did not know what to do.

I went to the kitchen and spoke with Steve and Jessie's mom. I was hesitating on whether I should call or not.

 Insight: With what I learned; I know now that the answer to that moment is CALL 988 even if you are not sure. Teens in the state of mind that she was in that night can't think about their well-being. They just want to be left alone. Leaving them alone is not an option.

Given what was going on, Jessie's mom said, *"I am going to do this easy for you, I will call 911. If she wants to be mad at someone, she can be mad at me for calling them"*.

The police arrived quickly after together with an ambulance.

The police knew our address well by this time. They visited our house many times for different reasons, all related to her condition. I remember before this instance, one night she just left the house past midnight. Daniel was sleeping, Sofia was in the kitchen, I was getting ready to sleep, and Steve was already in bed. I came out of our room to say goodnight and asked her to turn off the lights when she was done. I went to my room to finish up. When I was ready, maybe 20 minutes later, I went out of my room again to see if Sofia was done. The kitchen lights were still on. I went to her room to ask her to go back down to the kitchen and turn the lights off. She was not in her room.

After looking for her everywhere inside the house and the basement, I decided to call Steve up. *"Sofia is not in the house"*, I said nervously. *"What do you mean?"*, Steve replied. I looked for her and couldn't find her. The last time I saw her she was in the kitchen about 20 minutes ago. We both started the search. We looked again everywhere in the house and went outside this time.

I remember calling her out of the trees that she liked to climb. "If you are up on a tree and you are watching us, this is not funny. Please come down." There was no answer. We got so scared that we called the police. We were living the worst nightmare yet, calling the police to say that our teen was missing. Then comes that question that I was always afraid of being asked, "What was she wearing?". I could not say. "I saw her 20 minutes ago but I don't remember what she was wearing", I said. We described her the best we could and gave all the details over the phone to the officer in the case. I could not stop shaking.

The officer found Sofia 15-20 minutes after our call. She was walking back into the neighborhood when the police found her. We were in our yard when we saw the police car and the officer outside his car talking with her. She told the police, *"I just wanted to walk and take some fresh air and did not know about the curfew."* Sofia was not mean or malicious. I believed that she just wanted some fresh air. She just could not think of the consequences of her actions or how much we would worry about her. She felt like walking and she left.

Going back to the night when Jessie came to our house past midnight, the police started to ask questions of her. They were in her room because she was back there and did not want to come out. Jessie and his mom were still with us. After talking with Sofia, the police came out of her room and discussed with us the recommendation to take her to the hospital for evaluation. They said that it was our decision since the investigators were "*on the fence*" regarding sending her to the hospital. I went back into her room to check with Sofia. She started pleading with me again, "*I don't want to go back to the hospital. They don't help me and it is a waste of time. I don't want to miss school*".

While this was happening, an officer was outside the house talking some more with Jessie.

Two officers went back into Sofia's room to keep talking with her. I had found a video on her phone a couple of days prior and decided to show it to one of the officers. The one officer and I stepped out of the room. In this self-video, Sofia was contemplating whether or not she should jump off a bridge and into an interstate expressway near our house. It was filmed in the nighttime while on the said bridge. I remember thinking, "*Was that the night she went out for fresh air?*" In the video, she was talking to herself, "*If there is nothing after death, why not? Why not jump now? But what if there is something after we die?*" That day something stopped her and we got more time with her. I would never know if she took that video the night she disappeared on us or if it was at another time. It is frightening to realize that she left the house when we were possibly sleeping and she could have died that day.

As we were watching the video, news came through the police radio. "*Her friend says there is something prepared in her room to end her life*". We rushed to her room and we saw it. It was there the entire time while she was quietly sitting on her bed. At this point, Sofia was outside with some of the officers and an ambulance on standby. After seeing the video and finding the means to end her life, the police took over. They said it was not up to us anymore. She was heading to the hospital and we could not drive her as she was considered dangerous to self. We drove to the hospital in our car. Once in the hospital and after providing insurance information, we were informed that Sofia had asked to not let us go in to see her or be with her. I fought with the social worker but she said that Sofia's wishes came first and they needed her to feel safe. I felt betrayed by the system. She was a minor. The system wanted our financial data but I was not allowed to even go in for a few moments to see her. That was wrong on so many levels. I was in disbelief.

I was heartbroken for her. My poor Sofia Bella was not well and we were running out of options.

The hospital called us at about three in the morning. They said we could pick her up. I was confused. She was not doing well. What happened? Steve and I decided that we could not keep her safe in the house and therefore could not receive her right away. She needed help.

Sofia Bella was sent to a Behavioral Hospital once again. This was her third time. Once every month starting in August. The hospital released her 10 days after with an option to go into outpatient care. She refused. The order was not a mandate but a recommendation. One new med was added to her treatment. Sofia told me in our drive home, "*I just need to go back to school. That will make me feel much better ma'. I want to see my friends and catch up with my school work. This hospital was so much better than the ones before*". I took her for her outpatient evaluation. It did not seem that it was going to make a difference. I discussed options with her school's social worker. We all agreed that she was going back to school but had to report every day to the social worker's office to check in. Sofia agreed and so she went back to school.

Two weeks went by and she showed much progress. One morning I went to wake her up. I remember that morning so clearly. She opened her eyes big and closed them and opened them again doing this a few times, "*Ma', I think the medicine is working. I am sleeping better and I am feeling so much better*". I gave thanks to God for the work he was doing with her. My baby was getting better!

Thanksgiving came around. We had a beautiful time. Her sister was home and her aunt Brooke and uncle Jeff were there too. We took pictures and played family games as always and she participated contrary to the two years before. We celebrated her sister's birthday to close up the Thanksgiving celebrations.

Note left at her funeral by Jessie – "*I am so happy I got a chance to meet and come close with you. You may not know it but you saved me from so much. Whenever you yelled at me, I knew you cared. Thank you for letting me be a part of your life. … I'm so grateful that you were in mine and I'm sorry I couldn't save yours*".

I do not know if this is the last piece she wrote. But it is the last I am sharing with you before her closing poem, *A Glimpse of Heaven.*

Sofia's pencil portrait of Jessie.

Untitled

*maybe i never should have been born in the first place.
maybe i was just one big mistake— bringing pain to others
because of my mother's doing. maybe she was desperate,
and i was the result. i don't think i was ever meant to
grow into an adult. it's better to end it now while i'm
still young. squeeze the air out of my lungs. i wasn't
meant to be. let's make things right. end my strife. end
my deadly night. bring me the light that they say you see
right before you die. don't bother asking why when i'm
gone. just move on. think of it as a gift from me to you.
a final goodbye. a "see you soon."*

I felt deep sadness when I read this. I could not understand how she would think that she was an accident in the universe. My poor child. She was wanted before she was conceived. We loved watching her in our first sonogram and were full of joy and expectation when she started moving in my womb. We went bananas when we met her in the operating room with her angelic face and long eyelashes. My heart was full and the three of us; my older daughter, Steve, and I, were happy and anxious to bring her home. She completed our lives.

We corrected her when needed, taught her about God with words and deeds, and cheered her every step of the way. We loved that girl!

She knew of our love, but her mind was blurred.

CHAPTER 7

Our Baby is Gone

Death is inevitable. It is the only thing that is guaranteed in life. But it is not normal for parents to have to bury their children. I never expected to be one of the parents that would go through such a thing. Know this, God has a special heart for mourning parents. Uniting our suffering with that of Jesus at the cross is a special way to be united with Jesus in Heaven while we wait for our time to see our loved ones again. There is a special redemption in suffering with Jesus.

As you learned, Sofia Bella had many friends who loved her and cared for her, including those from middle school. She also had a lot of acquaintances at school and at work who admired her or were consoled by her. But when a teen is depressed, anxious, and becomes desperate, their view becomes very narrow. They don't see the big picture. They only know the pain of the moment. It becomes so unbearable that their brain tricks them into thinking that there is no other way to end the torment but to cut short their precious lives. In their minds, getting rid of the pain is all they can think about. They do not intend to cause pain to others. They are too gentle to want to hurt anyone by their actions.

"Fear not, for I have redeemed you; I have called you by name, you are mine. When you pass through the waters, I will be with you; and through the rivers, they shall not overwhelm you; when you walk through fire you shall not be burned and the flame shall not consume you. For I am the Lord your God."

Isaiah 43: 1-3 (NRSV)

Mom, Would You Pray for Sofia

I remember that Thanksgiving Day in 2021. Sofia Bella looked radiant and so full of life. The medicines seemed to be working and I felt grateful to God and everyone supporting her. She was dressed in black with a turtleneck, a bustier, a short cute black skirt, and fishnet stockings. I asked her to come outside with me for a picture. She came happily and even did a couple of poses for me. Her friend Bella came later with a homemade pumpkin pie, Sofia's favorite pie. I called Sofia after answering the door and she came running down the stairs like a gazelle. Sofia gave Bella a long, tight hug.

The previous week we heard Sofia a couple of times singing in her room and laughing at loud while talking with friends on the phone. I remember Steve and I looking at each other with a smile and a sigh of relief. Things were going to be okay.

Depression and anxiety are a roller coaster. You never know what event or thought can take you down a dark hole. One Sunday, almost a week and a half after Thanksgiving, an unexpected but familiar wave of anxiety came to my baby, and I was unable to sense it, let alone rescue her.

I was scheduled to fly on Monday, December 6, 2021, very early in the morning to visit my mom in Puerto Rico for her birthday, as I do every year. I always buy my ticket around February to make sure of getting a good price. Things were getting better therefore I decided to proceed with the plan. My mom also needed me and I wanted to see her. I asked Steve to drive me on Sunday night to the airport so that he could have a good night's sleep. I had to be at the airport by 3:30 in the morning.

Steve drove me to the airport at about 9:00 PM on Sunday, December

5th, 2021. During the ride to the airport, Steve was nervous about what could happen while I was visiting my mom. I was calm. I explained to him that Sofia was in God's hands and that everything was going to be well. I reminded him of the progress she had made and that I was going to be gone only for a few days. I could tell he was not at ease.

I thought, that if something happened, she would be taken to the hospital just like the last three times, she would be there for 10 days with no visits allowed, and by the end of the 10 days, I would be back home. I needed to see my mom. I left the car to go inside the airport. Something made me come back to the car. I opened the door and said, *"Steve, everything is going to be okay. I trust God that it will."*

At the airport, I made a couple of phone calls and then decided to listen to the next Bible in a Year session with Father Mike. I was behind on the program and going through the last of the Gospels. The chapter I was listening to was on Jesus' crucifixion. I received a call from home. It was Daniel saying, *"Dad says that you need to take a taxi home."* I thought *Sofia was heading to the hospital again.* I told Daniel that I needed to speak with Dad before I took a taxi back home. Daniel insisted and said, *"Mom, would you pray for Sofia?"* Daniel was asking me to pray for Sofia, maybe I should go back home. I went back home in a taxi while I made a couple of calls to Sofia's friends thinking that maybe they knew what was going on. I received short answers from friends. They knew something had happened earlier but they were not aware of Sofia's state at the time of my call. I prayed for Sofia Bella.

When I was 10 minutes away from the house, I called Steve to let him know that I was closer. It was at this time that I asked, *"How is Sofia doing? Was she taken to the hospital?"* *"Our baby is gone,"* Steve replied. *"Gone to the hospital?"* I asked. *"No honey. Our baby is dead"*, he replied as he started to cry.

Steve held the ambulance and made sure that I was able to see Sofia before she was taken. I will be forever grateful to Steve for holding them and to the Gurnee police for granting his request. I arrived at the house. The ambulance parked in front. I paid for the taxi and was led to enter the ambulance.

I saw my sweet girl *"sleeping"* on the stretcher. I was not mad at God. I was not looking for explanations. I knew where she was and that she was tormented no more. The first words out of my mouth were, *"Now you know what it is to go to Heaven. Did you see Jesus? You better be the first one in line to receive me when my time comes."*

I started kissing her and hugging her. I smelled her hair and kissed her some more. "*You washed your hair today baby. It smells so fresh*", I whispered in her ear. I must have kissed her over 200 times. I was not able to kiss that girl or get close to her in about 2-3 years.

The strength and confidence in God's providence when confronted with Sofia's death were the work of the Holy Spirit. I had surrendered her to God and His permissive will, and I trusted that what happened was the best for her. God did not want Sofia to die. But she did not want to keep living.

God did not want Sofia to die. But she
did not want to keep living.

I came to believe, through supernatural trust in God granted by the power of the Holy Spirit, that God allowed her death because she had endured way too much with her illness. Jesus said, "*I am with you always*" (Matthew 28:20). I know He was with Sofia Bella during her sleepless nights and drowsy days. Jesus knew her heart. He knew things were getting too overwhelming for her gentle soul. Jesus knew her desire to stop living and with much compassion heard her plead and took her by the hand as she drifted away. While other attempts failed, this one took her life.

On December 5, 2021, Sofia Isabella died by suicide late at night. Something happened that day between her and a friend. She felt sad thinking that her friend would never forgive her or talk to her again. She saw no way out but to finally leave this world.

No one is responsible for her death. She was very ill. Living with mental illness is a ride with unexpected drops and curves. That night the drop was lethal. We all tried so hard to help her according to what we knew and to the best of our abilities. God allowed her death at the end for reasons that I can't explain now but hope to one day understand.

I want to think that God in his infinite knowledge knew that things were not going to change but get worse. Filled with compassion for my child, God allowed her will to be done and took her into his arms. That is what my heart feels and it gives me comfort.

She is Broken No More

Sofia Bella was received into the embrace of Jesus' loving arms. I know this in my heart. The mysteries of the Father are revealed through the Holy Spirit to our hearts in many ways, and I have many stories to witness that my baby is in Heaven and suffers no more.

The same way we watched her as a baby in the nursery through a glass with our hearts full of love, we watched her through a glass at the cremation center. It came full circle.

She looked so pretty like Sleeping Beauty. Watching her lifeless body through the glass as she lay down was the most surreal moment of my life. Her gorgeous hair all fluffy around her face was glowing like rays of sun. Her lips were moisturized with a touch of lip balm, and her body was covered with a white sheet. She almost looked like a bride ready to meet Jesus. We spent half an hour talking to her, praying for her soul, and playing some music before she was pushed into cremation.

It was just Steve and I on our side of the glass and her on the other side. Laura Sambrano, our Funeral Director, was an angel sent by God to guide us through such a painful time. She gave us love, support, empathy, and all the time we needed alone with our baby. She also saved for us her digital prints and a beautiful lock of hair. When I could not think, Laura thought for me and made sure I was able to keep something so precious from her. I am grateful for her compassion and tender care of Sofia's body.

We were at peace during our last time with her body. There was no despair. We were grateful to God for 16 years of her amazing, curious, loving heart and mind. *"She was broken no more,"* my good friend Janet David said to me when I called her with the news.

I feel Sofia Bella closer to me than ever before. It sounds weird but it is so true. I know in my heart that she sees me and can better understand the deep love that we have for her.

Maybe one day I will write about all the beautiful signs God has given me of His love through the tragedy of her death and his reassurance that she is in Heaven like she always wanted to be.

Sofia Bella's poem on Heaven

Selfie of Sofia looking at the sun rising from her bedroom window. (2019)

A Glimpse of Heaven

Haven't you ever wondered

This peculiar question

That might just get you stumped:

"Does the universe ever end? And is there anything behind it?"

Scientists say it ends in darkness,

But that's not what I think.

It just can't be never ending darkness- at least it's not **dark**...

Well let me tell you, it does not,

For it just doesn't make any sense.

*What's behind that wall of **black**,*

Powdered sugar sprinkled on top?

No one really knows what is,

But let me tell you what I think-

*Behind that wall is **dreams** and **memories-***

But only the forgotten ones.
*If you broke that big **black** wall,*

And shattered all its stars,

Then behind it just might blind you-

Due to beauty and joy.

Hope overcomes you,

Drowning you in love,

Wishes embedded in your mind,

What no person's ever seen before…

You don't feel any pain,

Just the kind from joy,

Like a clone of heaven.

This is lost in s p a c e.

Oh, that fire, burning in your soul,

Just seething you with the kind of anger that you've never felt before.

Everything just like a dream,

The best one you've ever had.

The space crew ask you questions,

Frantic with excitement are they,

But you tone them out with goodness at your side.

All you hear is laughter.

Not only lost in space,

But Happiness and time and everything in between.

Tons of visions like no other.

Lives of many people flash before you-

Their memories and hopes, wishes and dreams.

You wish you could stay forever, but time blocks your visit.

Limited time do you have

To spend in such a place-

Only a few minutes to experience glory.

So as the memories fade away, one by one, leaving you,

images melting, you realize it's time

To go back home to a place called Earth.

You're slowly being p u l l e d

Back into Reality

Fingers being torn away

From the beautiful Place you'll never see again

You force a tear to not be released,

But at the same time

A smile escapes from your lips-

The only bit of Happiness that stays with you.

And when you've returned,

To Earth, your home,

You're telling everyone about your Journey-

Feeling better than ever before.

And when you sink into your couch when the day is finished,

*And the **dark** mask of night consumes the land,*

Only one thing goes through your mind:

"I've just took a visit to Heaven."

This is the last picture I took of my Sofia. It was on Thanksgiving Day, November 26, 2021. Only nine days before she decided to leave everything behind. Suicidal Doesn't Always Look Suicidal – Campaign Against Living Miserably (CALM) at thecalmzone.net

Final Thoughts

I cannot describe my pain. A piece of me died with her passing. Sofia Bella grew in the depths of my womb and developed into a smart, caring, happy person who was transformed little by little into someone who saw herself as inconsequential. In the eyes of many, she was a ray of light, but she only saw herself as a cloudy aching storm.

I am not sorry for Sofia Bella. I am sorry for myself and for those missing her deeply. She is at peace now with no worries, no sadness, no constant state of anxiety trying to rob her free-spirited joy. We are the ones drowning in questions and wanting explanations.

Did she know how much I loved her? That is a question that I will always ask myself when thinking about her. I want to believe that deep inside she did. But my love for her was not something that she pondered or thought about in her moment of unbearable distress. I want to believe that she knew deep inside that I would love her no matter what. I surely told her that truth many times.

I know that at times she saw me as her enemy. I tried so hard to be the mom I thought she would want me to be while trying to keep her safe. This was hard and probably unattainable. This world and all its distractions and distorted ideas of "happiness" break souls and leave them hopeless.

Social media bombards us with all kinds of lies. "*Do what feels good.*" "*If it makes you happy, then it is ok.*" "*It is your body, do whatever, nobody should care.*" These are only a few of the many lies spread out to harm our minds. The truth is that we are made to be loved by God and be in love with him. We are made to live in community, not alone minding our own business. We are to help each other, cry with each other, and celebrate each other.

We are made to be loved by God and be in love with him.

We consume too much social media and allow ourselves to be guided by pop culture expectations. These expectations become our roadmap, yet they are far from the reality of who we are: sons and daughters of God made to live eternal lives with our Heavenly Father.

The so-called "influencers" impose expectations that many times drive us to isolation, loneliness, and desperation. All these negative feelings come when we find ourselves not fitting the "expected" part. These pressures can drive anyone into hopeless despair. Imagine what it can do to young sensitive minds. In many cases, all these factors drive our teens into believing that they don't matter and that no one cares about them. Soon these ideas become too loud in their minds and drive them to think that the best solution is to be gone by suicide.

If you want to be an agent of change and make a difference in the lives of the young people around you, read helpful books or websites to understand mental health and kids' developmental stages. More on Chapter 8.

If you are in the middle of the storm, find a helpful support group or create one for yourself with friends, family, and your church community. Ask God for guidance by spending time in prayer, telling Him what is going on and what you want to see change. Of course, God knows already what you want, but it helps you to express it and it makes for a good dialogue with God. It is in relationship and sharing with God that I found many of the answers to my questions. He loves you and He cares.

 Insight: Read the Bible. Following the Bible in a Year with Father Mike Schmitz was helpful for me while I was going through the storm and fighting to keep her alive. It gave me a better understanding of Christian life and why bad things happen to good people. The Book of Job and Father Mike's explanations were a critical component in helping me understand our situation. The Word of God through the Holy Bible helped me grow in my love for those around me and in patience to deal with the challenges I faced. When she was gone, the words in the Bible consoled me and gave me a new perspective and hope.

Finally, do what your heart tells you is right. You know your teen better than anyone. No ONE path works for everyone. You need to create your own. The most important thing is to DO WHAT YOU THINK

IS BEST trusting that God will be with you supporting you and your teen as the loving Father that He is. Whatever happens, after doing all this, you can find peace in knowing that you did your best. There is no better feeling in **triumph or a seeming defeat** than the satisfaction that comes from knowing you did all you could and that you did it with love and compassion.

No ONE path works for everyone. You need to create your own.

Remember what Jesus promised:

"I am with you always."

Matthew 28:20 (NRSV)

*Sofia Bella immersed in her thoughts while strolling along a
Lake Michigan pier in Waukegan, IL. Summer 2021.*

CHAPTER 8

Getting Ready for Battle

Prepare to Fight a Good Fight

You are probably asking, now what? How do I fight with strength yet not lose myself in the process or hurt my child even more? If you are dealing with a teen suffering from mental illness, you are probably scared, a little bit ashamed, and in total disbelief. How did we get here? What happened to my loving, caring child?

So much happened. Some things you knew were coming, like the hard years of adolescence, the fight for independence, and the normal process of defining who they are away from you. Other things you suspected could happen but never thought they would happen to you. *"We are different." "We are paying attention." "We are vigilant and know his friends." "We care and set boundaries,"* I said all these things to myself many times. Yet, it happened to me.

Sofia Bella carried a lot of pain. She never did drugs or alcohol, and I am very proud of her for that. That would have complicated things even more. I now know she was hurting, scared, and trying to get attention in one way or another. I am not a mental health professional but I now understand that the little child inside of her was scared and saw no other way out. Regardless of the resources she had available and the people who wanted to help her, she walked on a self-destructive path with the belief that life was "a nothing" that added to "nada" so why keep living?

Based on my experience, the first help we need to get is for ourselves. If you ever took a flight and paid attention to the instructions from your flight attendant, you know that if the oxygen level drops in the cabin, you need to put on your oxygen mask first and then help others around you. If you are not well, you can help no one. I became so preoccupied with her and what she would need to be better, happier, and "normal," that I overlooked figuring out what I needed to achieve that goal. I did not take the time to better understand what I was fighting against. "I ran out of oxygen" and became tired and hopeless.

There are no maps, protocols, procedures, or books that can give you all the answers to your specific situation. There is a saying that goes like this, "*kids do not come with an instruction manual.*" At least at the beginning of their lives, we can pretty much get by with what we know and quickly learn how to keep them warm, fed, and developing well for the most part. Once they get into the neighborhood of their teen years, the game changes and becomes more complicated.

In addition to what you've done so far to help your child thrive, you now need to consider unexpected consequences of hormonal changes, complex brain development issues, challenges against authority, friends becoming their source of trust and truth instead of your good intentions and experience, and many other things. On top of what normally happens, pure biology and behavioral science, add the possible use of alcohol and drugs, a culture of instant gratification where things are "now or never," "all or nothing," online relationships that lack human interaction and can be cruel, and thousands upon thousands of options to distract and numb their minds. It is a very hard and sad reality for many parents.

What can you do then? Prepare for the "battle." Start early. Do not wait until you are in the middle of the war to see what tools are available to you. This requires work, discipline, and time away from your distractions and duties. Do not sit back and relax thinking that it will not happen to you because it can and you need to be prepared. You do not need to be an expert but know where to go and what to look for.

The same tools that can destroy our kids, social media and digital resources, can help us prepare. There are a lot of parents out there who are hurting, struggling, trying to find answers, and trying to keep their children alive, just like you. Find them. Reach out.

There are many podcasts, YouTube videos, and social media groups discussing mental health and other related topics that could be affecting your teen. All of these tools, in moderation, can help you develop the awareness and curiosity that you will need to create a plan to support your teen in whatever direction their development takes them. Listen to parents who fought this battle before you did. Gain from their experience so that you can have a fighting chance when the time comes. If you do all the work, and you end up not needing it, be thankful to God. Use your knowledge to help others. So many parents feel hopeless and desperate. I did!

Use my experience to work to your benefit. I am going to cite some resources that I found useful. Many of them, I discovered after the fact. I want to share them with you because I think these could have been helpful back when I was trying so desperately to fight for my teen. Many of them were "oxygen masks" that I should have put on before attempting to help my precious Sofia Bella.

Things I learned:

1. Not having medical insurance that covers mental health is a nightmare. I went through that hell and back.

2. Not all mental health professionals are created equal. Find the one that matches your kid's personality and who stays a step ahead of her/him instead of being passive waiting for your child to open up. Sofia Bella outplayed them by saying what they needed to hear and they went along with it - especially if that meant getting herself out of the system/hospital faster.

3. Your teen needs face-to-face care. Telehealth is not as effective and face-to-face needs to include the family at some point.

4. Your teen will tell you all kinds of things. "*I am fine.*" "*I will never kill myself.*" Sofia Bella said those things to me. They don't mean to lie. Their emotions and thoughts change quickly and what they feel today is not what they will feel tomorrow. Keep checking. Use your

instincts. Also, know that with all the care in the world, things may turn out differently from what you expect or wish. Mental Health is very unpredictable.

5. Breathe! Breathe again! Breathe some more. You must remain calm so you can think more clearly. I developed a habit of running/ walking in the afternoons. It helped me to do something for myself. It kept my mind clear, my heart loving, and my approach to Sofia Bella less judgmental as my stress levels were down after my exercise. Maybe you can't run, find something that you love doing that will positively recharge your energy. Sometimes, just getting fresh air and spending time in nature is all that is needed.

6. Hold on to faith in God's love and his divine providence. It makes a difference! I listened to the program *Bible in a Year* with Father Mike Schmitz. This program is for Catholics and Non-Catholics. It helped me better understand many things regarding life, brokenness, and evil in this world. It also landed me in many serious conversations and even arguments with God, blowing off some steam and bringing me closer to our Heavenly Father. Faith was an important aspect that helped me with my struggles battling Sofia Bella's sickness. Faith was even more crucial to deal with the aftermath of her death by suicide. If you think you do not have time to read the Bible, think again. This is a program where you hear Scriptures and they are explained and applied to real life by Father Mike in 20-30 minutes a day chunks. Father Mike was in my ears as I walked/ran or did my chores at home. Find the *Book of Job* in the Bible. Better yet, find the portion of *Bible in a Year* with Father Mike where the Book of Job is read and discussed. Father Mike's explanation was good in helping me understand why sometimes bad things happen to good people and why we can still trust God regardless of the bad things that happen in our lives. I promise it will be very helpful.

7. Listen to music that nourishes your soul. You can choose instrumental music or Christian songs. Music is a balm to the soul. There are many types of Christian songs. Some of them are uplifting, others talk to our pain and desperation while giving us the hope

that comes when we hold on to God through our hardships. Some of my favorites are: *Perfectly Loved* by Rachael Lampa, *God, Turn It Around* by Jon Reddick, *Who I Am* by Ben Fuller, *Hold On, Please*, and *In Jesus' Name* by Katy Nichole, and *Look What You've Done* by Tasha Layton. I am sure you can find other songs that will mean the world to you as you go through this difficult journey. Make a playlist with your favorites and listen to it frequently.

Resources I wish I had discovered earlier.

1. If there is an urgent mental health crisis needing immediate assistance, call 911 or reach out to the National Suicide Prevention hotline by calling or texting **988 or** by going to: 988lifeline.org. "The 988 Lifeline is a national network of local crisis centers that provides free and confidential emotional support to people in suicidal crisis or emotional distress 24 hours a day, 7 days a week in the United States. They are committed to improving crisis services and advancing suicide prevention by empowering individuals, advancing professional best practices, and building awareness" (988lifeline.org).

2. Read *The Suicide Prevention Pocket Book – How to Support Someone Who is Having Suicidal Feelings* by Joy Hibbins. Hibbins is the founder and CEO of the charity Suicide Crisis

3. *Hope and Healing for Kids Who Cut* is a good and easy-to-read book on dealing with self-harming. There are many other books as well.

4. The National Alliance Mental Illness (NAMI) organization is the largest grassroots mental health organization dedicated to building better lives for the millions of Americans affected by mental illness. It started as a small group of families gathered around a kitchen table in 1979 whose loved ones were suffering from mental illness and were not well represented or advocated for. It is now the nation's leading voice on mental health. They are an alliance of more than 600 local affiliates who work in different communities

to raise awareness and provide support and education that was not previously available to those in need. Their website has a wealth of resources. It is a great place to start. Their website is www.nami.org. Go under the *Support & Education* tab. Look for the *Circle of Care Guidebook: A Guidebook for Mental Health Caregivers.* Another very helpful tab is *About Mental Illness*, click on *Warning Signs and Symptoms*. Their video *10 Common Warning Signs of a Mental Health Condition* can be found on their website or a YouTube search. NAMI's website has resources in Spanish as well.

5.   Substance Abuse and Mental Health Services Administration known as SAMHSA is another website with many resources specifically when substance use is part of the problem.

6.   Mental Health America, MHA, will provide resources and ways to connect with others. They also offer Mental Health screenings that can help detect symptoms before is too late.

7.   The next resource is an app, Parenting Today's Teens with Mark Gregston. Some Podcast titles to look for are *Teens and Depression: Stopping the Spiral, The Value of Admitting Our Struggles,* and *Don't Miss THIS Cry for Help.* There are so many good topics. All their sessions are very educational. They present real-life cases and provide strategies to deal with teens in a healthy way that builds parent/teen relationships. Every so often, they interview teens who had struggled before and are doing better. You hear their stories and what happened that changed their path to a more constructive one. Very revealing!

8.   Relevant Radio is a Catholic radio program. Relevant Radio can be accessed via their app or website via www.Relevantradio.com. There is one particular show that deals with many challenging topics including topics that affect teens. Particularly interesting is Trending with Timmerie. Her program on February 24, 2023, talked about the dangers of smartphones, social media, and suicide in girls. The title of that show is *Solutions for Relationships & Suffering Teen Girls.* In that particular show, the host of Trending with Timmerie

discusses with Melanie Hempe, from www.ScreenStrong.com, how smartphones impact relationship satisfaction and what to do about it. For that topic, check the recording at 3:56 minutes into the show. At 24:07 minutes into the show, Melanie discusses the latest CDC report about teenage girls, their suffering, and what to do.

9. Smart phones, screen time, and everything that comes with it are damaging our kids. Many experts are associating smartphones given to pre-teens as one of the most damaging things a parent can do to sabotage their relationship with their kids and start them up on a path that can lead to low self-esteem, mental illness, and self-destruction. Screen Strong is an organization dedicated to educating parents about the risks of screen time and how to create environments that are conducive to better mental health for teens and happier families. Go to www.ScreenStrong.org and locate the tab Resources on the top of the page, scroll down to *Screen Addiction - Research and Statistics*. It will blow your mind away. You will find a course on *Kids' Brains & Screens* that has very valuable information. Quote from their website; "*We've done our best to compile a robust amount of information, articles, and research studies on a variety of topics.*" Education on this topic will give you better ways to battle this terrible plague that is affecting the lives of too many kids. They also have a blog and a podcast by the same name, ScreenStrong.

10. Suicide Prevention Resource Center (SPRC). SPRC is the only federally supported resource center devoted to advancing the implementation of the National Strategy for Suicide Prevention. SPRC is funded by the U.S. Department of Health and Human Services' Substance Abuse and Mental Health Services Administration (SAMHSA). Their website is www.sprc.org.

11. Cognitive Behavioral Therapy or CBT is not a website but something good to know and look into. Cognitive Behavioral Therapy (CBT) is a form of psychological treatment that has been demonstrated to be effective for a range of problems including depression, anxiety disorders, alcohol and drug use problems, marital problems, eating disorders, and severe mental

illness. Numerous research studies suggest that CBT leads to significant improvement in functioning and quality of life. In many studies, CBT has been demonstrated to be as effective as, or more effective than, other forms of psychological therapy or psychiatric medications. Go here for more information www.apa.org/ptsd-guideline/patients-and-families/cognitive-behavioral.

12. CAMS-CARE.org - "There are three evidence-based (randomized controlled trials) interventions and treatments that are designed to directly target suicide risk. These interventions have demonstrated effectiveness in reducing suicidality in general, as well as significantly reduce suicide attempts, increase hope and reasons for living and improve clinical retention" (see *cams-care.org*). They are Collaborative Assessment and Management of Suicidality (CAMS), Dialectical Behavior Therapy (DBT), and Cognitive Behavioral Therapy (CBT), but specifically Suicide Prevention (CT-SP) and Brief CBT.

13. Find a therapist who is trained in CAMS—Collaborative Assessment and Management of Suicidality. "*CAMS is a treatment framework in which a client and a clinician work together to keep the patient stable, ideally in outpatient therapy, and identifies the "drivers" that compel the client to take their life.*" The therapist and the client work on treating those drivers to reduce stress, hopelessness, and suicidal ideation while increasing hope. Clinical research shows that clients like the CAMS Framework® and are more likely to remain in treatment using CAMS. CAMS is "Well Supported as a clinical intervention for suicidal ideation per CDC criteria and is proven to reduce suicidal ideation in as few as 6 sessions with a trained therapist." (www.cams-care.org)

14. Suicide Awareness Voices of Education (SAVE) is another good source of information. Their website is www.save.org - SAVE was one of the nation's first organizations dedicated to the prevention of suicide. Their work is based on the foundation and belief that suicide could be preventable and everyone has a role to play in preventing suicide. Through raising public awareness, educating communities, and equipping every person with the right tools, they want to SAVE lives.

15. QPR is an approach to mental health emergencies just like the CPR program is for cardiac events. The CPR process is designed to stabilize people who aren't breathing or breathing intermittently and who may be in cardiac arrest until the person can reach a hospital or other care. Similarly, QPR is an emergency mental health intervention for persons with suicidal thoughts. QPR represents the process itself; **Question, Persuade, and Refer**. The intent is to identify and interrupt the crisis and direct that person to the proper care. Please go to www.qprinstitute.com to learn more.

16. Catholic Charities has a Loving Outreach to Survivors of Suicide program known as the LOSS program. This program was extremely helpful to me in dealing with the aftermath of suicide.

Just Had to Say it Again

Parents or caregivers, please understand this: depression with suicidal thoughts, self-harming, and other unwanted behaviors are not necessarily the result of bad environments, bad experiences, or poor parenting. Sometimes it just happens. This is why we should all educate ourselves on mental health, how it manifests, and where to go for help. I think this should be a conversation at annual checkups for pre-teens and through their teen years. Doctors sometimes ask vaguely or as a routine question. You need to ask the questions too. *"Have you felt depressed lately?"* *"Have you thought or know someone who has talked about suicide?"* If you suspect, ask! It is well known in the field of psychology that asking someone if they have suicidal thoughts does not give the person ideas to die by suicide. This is a myth.

Have the strength to ask honest questions without an agenda or the fear of not knowing how to respond. It is fine to say *"I don't know how to answer to that, but I love you and we will figure it out together."* Attend a **QPR training** (mentioned above) to learn other helpful ways to ask and respond.

Insight: Places that provide services or work with pre-teens or teens should have workshops around identifying people at risk and how to converse with them. <u>Presenting slides with information without providing time to practice conversations that go to the root of the problem is useless.</u> Push for more. We practice how to take orders when we work in a fast-food place. This is way more important and requires practice to loosen up and have the courage to engage our teens in asking tough questions. Be ready and have confidence. Talk to them! Once you engage, if you feel it's warranted or if in doubt, refer them to a mental health professional at school or elsewhere depending on the case.

 Insight: Schools and health care professionals - don't just give families and teens a pamphlet to read. Encourage parents by asking a question or two and increasing their curiosity to find out more about the subject and educate themselves.

Most importantly, do not dismiss this issue as if it is *"just part of being a teen."* We are losing too many of them. We can't afford to lose more young lives to suicide.

Call To Action

If this book helps you or anyone you know in any way, please let me know. You can share your story by sending us an email at authorMariaMartina@gmail.com. I will then better understand the purpose of Sofia Bella's untimely death. Her seed would have given fruit, and that is what this tribute is all about.

My plea with you, reader, is that you share this book with as many as possible; parents, teachers, and other adults who might benefit from reading it. The book is available on paper cover and as an e-reader.

In loving memory of Sofia Isabella Wexler,
*please **help yourself or a friend.***

LOVE *yourself and* SHARE *your story.*

BOOK CLUB QUESTIONS

Questions about the book in general

1. What was the intent or objective of Between Love and Grief – A Mother's Journey After Teen Suicide?

2. How do you rate your awareness of mental health and suicide prevention before reading the book on a scale of 1 to 10 where "1" is very poor and "10" is very aware of details. After reading the book, how do you rate yourself?

3. What was surprising about the facts contained in this book? Why was it surprising?

4. What section or element of the book had the most impact on you? Was it good or bad? Share parts of that section and its impact.

5. Did the way the book was written affect your enjoyment or ability to understand the subject? Give examples.

6. Did your opinions on the subject change due to information contained in this book? Has your interest in the subject matter increased? How so?

7. What "life lesson" can be learned from this story? Was your outlook changed positively or negatively? Explain.

8. What is your final impression of the book as a whole? Has it changed your views on teen mental health and suicide prevention?

Personal questions for journaling

1. Thinking about the teens in your life, write two things that were presented in the book that were different from what you knew or believed.

2. Did this book make you reconsider the way you interact with teens? Would you do anything differently? Why or why not?

3. What is your main concern or preoccupation with the teens in your life right now?

4. What do you think is getting in the way of your relationship with the teen in your life? What can you do to change that?

ACKNOWLEDGEMENT

T hank you to everyone who was part of our journey with Sofia Isabella. For the ones who listened, consoled, and prayed with me and for her while my baby was struggling; THANK YOU. May our precious Lord give you support and hope for your struggles. Know that I will continue my prayers for all of you. I know that many of you are still praying for her soul.

Neighbors, friends, and even strangers - the outpouring of your love and mercy at the time of Sofia Isabella's death and the months after gave me strength. My soul was comforted by your words and acts of kindness towards our family. I never felt alone. As I felt the spiritual love of God in my heart, you were the hands and feet of Jesus sustaining us, feeding us, and helping financially to take care of Sofia Isabella's funeral arrangements. Praise and thank you Jesus for your generosity of heart.

I want to give special thanks to two beautiful and caring ladies in our family, Valeria and Brooke. Their love for Sofia Isabella was unconditional and deep. It made my momma heart grateful. These two beautiful souls dropped everything to be with us only hours after the terrible news. They took charge of preparing the details for her Life Celebration and Funeral Mass and made it with exquisite taste and loving care to ensure that it would fit Sofia Isabella's taste and liking. In a time when I could barely think, they came up with gorgeous flower arrangements, masterful posters depicting her life, and video memories to run at the church for the enjoyment of all who came to give us their condolences. Jeff and Eric, thank you for supporting them. I was in awe of everything you all created through such a difficult time for all of us. We love you dearly and will be forever grateful.

Finally, thank you to all of those who provided feedback to make this book possible. There are too many names, and I am afraid I will miss someone if I try to list you all. Special thanks to those who were total strangers and donated their time and talents to the editing and the suggesting of ideas. May God bless you all with abundant graces.

She confidently trusts the LORD to take care of her.

Psalm 112:7

ABOUT
THE AUTHOR

Maria-Martina Maldonado is a suicide loss survivor and author of *Between Love and Grief: A Mother's Journey After Teen Suicide*. Since losing her daughter, Sofia Bella, to suicide it has become her mission to help other parents who have teens struggling with mental health through her story. If you are a parent whose child has shown symptoms of suicidal ideation, use the QR code below to connect and join our community of support.

www.ingramcontent.com/pod-product-compliance
Lightning Source LLC
Chambersburg PA
CBHW070707130626
46553CB00005B/1874